INCREASE SALES WITHOUT LEAVING YOUR DESK

Edmund Tirbutt

KOGAN
PAGE

First published in 1991

Apart from any fair dealing for the purposes of research or private study,
or criticism or review, as permitted under the Copyright, Designs and
Patents Act, 1988, this publication may only be reproduced, stored or
transmitted, in any form or by any means, with the prior permission in
writing of the publishers, or in the case of reprographic reproduction in
accordance with the terms of licences issued by the Copyright Licensing
Agency. Enquiries concerning reproduction outside those terms should
be sent to the publishers at the undermentioned address:

Kogan Page Limited
120 Pentonville Road
London N1 9JN

© Edmund Tirbutt and Kogan Page Limited

British Library Cataloguing in Publication Data

A CIP record for this book is available from the British Library.

ISBN 0-7494-0183-4
ISBN 0-7494-0184-2 Pbk

Printed and bound in Great Britain by
Clays Limited, St Ives plc

Contents

Introduction

Business owners and managers often see their primary roles as producers, to the detriment of sales. It cannot be emphasised too heavily that, in market-led firms, if there are no customers, all too soon there is no business either. Success depends largely on a regular flow of orders and prompt cash collection.

Since the need is to achieve maximum sales with the least effort and at minimum cost, the manager's organising skills and ability to motivate his staff are vital factors in gaining business and increasing market share. Modern communication technology allows high sales to be achieved and close customer contact maintained using fewer sales people on the road.

Once a sales plan has been prepared, and targets set, in consultation with your staff, it remains to check that the necessary equipment is available for its implementation. The owner/manager can mastermind the sales from the office, at the same time monitoring production and service departments.

The telephone, the post, advertising and PR all have entire chapters devoted to them, and a wealth of detail is provided on how innovative devices and operations can be effectively deployed and important sources of further information contacted. Costs are quoted and compared throughout. The advantages of using external organisations to obtain publicity are explored through real-life case studies.

The days when the only way to make a sale was a face-to-face call have gone. Those who have problems leaving their desks now have a wide variety of tried and tested sales methods from which to choose.

1
Behind the Sale Strategy

The closing of any sale represents the tip of a massive iceberg. The powers of persuasion of the sales person are merely one of numerous important ingredients that make a sale. The considerations that motivate consumers to buy, continue buying and consequently recommend a product are many and various.

It has long been established that a good sales person with a bad product will outsell a bad sales person with a good product. But good sales people are few and far between and are unlikely to remain long with an organisation that cannot offer the products their skills deserve. Furthermore, the act of selling people unsatisfactory goods is invariably counter-productive. Profit margins are so very much tighter when there are no repeat business and referrals and nothing is more easily established than a bad reputation.

A good product will play a major part in selling itself. If it is attractively priced and readily available the calibre of an organisation's sales force becomes less important.

Many of the decisions you will need to make can be made without having to leave your desk. Let us examine some of the principal areas that need to be considered.

Accessibility

The sales person out on the road derives much of his or her success from physical presence. People tend to buy from him or her because he or she is there. They are nearly always buying the person rather than the product although the process is subconscious. When they seek to place further orders or to make recommendations to friends and colleagues the sales person's appearance and personality will spring readily to mind.

Because you will not be leaving your desk you do not have this advantage, but there are many steps that you can take to make your products easier to sell and help your company and your goods to be remembered.

Credit cards

Many people wish to make instant purchases. Some needs must be satisfied immediately and many propositions are irresistible. It is in such situations that the very least amount of selling is necessary. But the sale can only be completed if the customer is able to pay. By accepting credit cards as a means of payment a business person can go a long way towards solving the customer's immediate funding problem and the money is safe and quickly available. A sale can be made by merely recording an identifying number. This means that a transaction can even be completed over the telephone or by fax.

Every card has its own unique number which relates to its carrier and in turn to his or her credit limit. Carriers have accounts with credit card companies. By volunteering their numbers they invite a business to debit their account. At the point of sale the business can easily verify, by means of a simple phone call to the relevant credit card company, that there is enough credit available on the account to cover the purchase.

Any business unable to make use of such a facility is, among other things, depriving itself of some of the easiest sales that it will ever make. The two most widely used credit cards are Visa and MasterCard. The process of applying for the facility to offer both of these is straightforward. Dial 0800 616161. No charge will be made for the call. Your basic details such as your name, address, type of business and average transaction value will be taken down over the phone. Information will subsequently be sent to you through the post and in some cases a representative will visit your office. The combined joining fee for both cards is £50. From then onwards you pay a 4 per cent service charge on the volume of business you transact. For other cards, such as those offered by Diners Club and American Express, separate applications are necessary to the organisations concerned.

The use of credit cards has grown rapidly during recent years. Indeed, in many areas of business their availability has become a prerequisite for trade to take place at all. The facility can be used to play an important part in overall sales and marketing strategy. Many of the methods for increasing your sales described in

Chapters 2 to 7 cannot be exploited to their full potential unless credit cards are accepted.

Enabling a customer to buy immediately and pay later is one of the most effective devices available for prompting him or her into action.

Company name

The significance of a company's name is commonly underestimated. A shrewd choice can do as much to increase sales as many long months of planning or canvassing. If a name can arouse initial interest and be easily remembered it can provide a company with a clear superiority over its competitors and even attract a great many new customers into an industry.

Many people seeking a product or service with which they are not as yet familiar scan Yellow Pages or their Thomson Local Directory to find an initial point of contact. They are normally presented with an embarrassment of riches. A name that stands out from the crowd can work wonders in gaining their attention. A sole trader who styles himself 'Peter Fleeter', for example, is likely to stimulate considerably more interest than one who uses the title 'P J Fleeter'.

Few businesses are fortunate enough to boast household names, but those that operate with names that readily spring to mind have a clear advantage over those that don't. Names should be kept short if they are to be easily remembered – no more than three or four syllables. A long name may create a striking first impression, but is difficult to remember. Words that rhyme and those that contain unusual imagery are also easily recalled. Strong concrete references to everyday phenomena such as 'Sky' or 'Land' are far more likely to be remembered than abstract phrases. But do avoid using acronyms – those infuriating letters – and try instead a name that is descriptive of your product or service. For example, The Pentonville Bargain Tyre Company is more likely to pull in sales than a company called TPBTC Ltd.

Telephone number

Do not restrict your imagination to the names under which you trade. Extend it to your telephone. If your telephone number is easy to remember you will be readily available even to those who cannot recall your company's exact name. You do not have to continue with your allotted number. British Telecom will attempt to change it for you to suit your requirements. Unless the request is for something particularly unusual, such as 666 666, the service will not normally cost more than the standard charge for changing a number – about £25.

If possible, try to get your phone number to rhyme or to be directly associated with yourself or your company's name. If you cannot find a direct link try to opt for something that is purely and simply unusual. People are far more likely to remember a number such as 363 3600 than they are one such as 429 8071. You may well find that many of the numbers that you think up can't be granted. But a little bit of trial and error could well pay substantial dividends. It may also prove fun to do.

Your logo – the company's flag

A good company logo can do much to raise a firm's profile. Try to think of a symbol that can be readily associated with your organisation and use it in all your advertising and promotional literature. It must be easily identifiable to the extent that it is capable of attracting attention when surrounded by other visual material. It must also be easily reproducible. You will need it to appear on material of greatly differing size and variety. It must be small enough to fit on your business card but interesting enough to create the desired impression in large advertisements. Most effective logos do not actually incorporate the name of the organisation concerned within the symbol that is chosen. They concentrate instead on the ease with which the two can be connected.

A good logo is worth money to a business. It is probably worth getting a professional designer to produce one for you, rather than rely on your own amateur efforts.

Trade marks

Devising a distinctive phrase or symbol by which your goods are described can readily distinguish your products from those of your competitors and greatly increase the chances that consumers will remember what you have to offer. Just think of the brand names that come to mind when you are making a purchase – Ever Ready for a battery, Wonderloaf if you like sliced bread. The need for a good trade mark is all the more important for those firms operating in markets where a large number of competitors offer broadly the same products at similar prices.

Once you have devised a suitable trade mark you would be well advised to ensure that it is officially registered. By doing so you will obtain sole rights over its ownership for seven years. These can be renewed indefinitely. A registered owner has recourse to legal action for infringement of his or her rights.

A trade mark must meet certain standards to qualify for registration. It must:

1. Be distinctive in itself. In general this means that it should not describe in any way the product that it relates to or involve the use of non-distinctive expressions which other traders may reasonably wish to use in the course of trade.
2. Not attempt to deceive the customer.
3. Not be confusable with the trade mark of a similar product already registered.

Each application for registration must specify the particular goods in respect of which registration is sought. All goods are classified into one or other of 34 different categories. Services cannot be registered. Applications are checked for suitability in the Trade Marks Registry. If they are considered to be prima facie acceptable for registration details are published in the *Trade Marks Journal*. A month is allowed to elapse during which it is open to any person who objects to give notice of opposition to the registration.

Information on how to set about registering a trade mark can be obtained from:

The Registrar
The Patent Office
Trade Marks Registry
State House
66–71 High Holborn
London WC1R 4TP

Choosing your product

The reasons why people buy are many and varied. Some are intent on following the latest fashions while others are motivated by a desire to obtain the best that is available. An urge for self-improvement and a feeling that value for money is being secured are other powerful motivating forces. The combination of such factors, along with many others, varies noticeably from one individual to another. Nervertheless, all consumers have one essential purchasing habit in common – they buy for their own reasons and not for yours!

So it is vital to determine the levels of demand that are present in the market-place before deciding on suitable products to sell. Far too many businesses begin by establishing what their resources permit them to make or obtain and then see whether or not their decisions are justified by sales. Always think in terms of what you can do to satisfy people's existing needs rather than trying to create new ones. That way, you will make more profit more quickly.

Studies of competitors can shed much light on the buoyancy of the markets in which they operate. Firms do not stay in business for long periods by accident, and only expand into new areas when they believe there is a good reason to do so. Analyse carefully the products offered by your opposition. Try to gain a clear idea in your own mind as to why they are proving successful. See if you can think of ways of improving them. Further vital information on demand potential can be obtained from the market research methods outlined below.

When, and only when, you have established that a market for your products exists should you turn your attention to the more intricate issues involved with their production and promotion. Your primary objective should be to ensure that you provide items of sufficient quality to obtain high levels of repeat business and widespread recommendation. Goods should provide your clientele with positive benefits that will become apparent after purchase as well as with selling points that persuade them to buy in the first place.

You must believe in what you are offering. If you don't, the public is most unlikely to do so. If you have come up with the right product you should know exactly why people will want to buy from you rather than from your competitors. Try to devise your own *unique selling points* (USPs). These will be particularly useful when it comes to advertising or selling via the post and telephone. Make sure, however, that any claims you make to being unusual are strictly realistic.

How to set the price

The prices that you charge will to a certain extent be determined by the costs you incur. There is no point in being in business unless the price you charge for your goods and services provides you with a genuine chance of making a profit. The amount which the consumer is prepared to pay is also a major determining factor. A healthy profit margin is useless if people are unwilling to pay the price being asked.

There is no such thing as a standard formula for setting prices. Even the largest companies use a high degree of instinct in their pricing policies. Of the many factors involved, however, the prices charged by competitors should always figure prominently. Sales estimates and cash flow forecasts also have an important part to play.

If in doubt there is much to be said for experimenting with a price which could prove too high than with one which may turn out to be too low. It can be lowered if demand fails to be satisfactory. If a product is exceptionally cheap the consumer is often suspicious of its quality. The *perceived value* of a product is very important. The ability to offer discounts is also greatly reduced and profit margins can be squeezed to the extent that unexpected setbacks become major catastrophes.

If due consideration is given to developing unique selling points the need to be the cheapest in the market-place becomes less urgent. Trying to establish superiority on price alone is often a dangerous game to play. Prices in any industry are subject to constant fluctuations and larger competitors can reduce their prices overnight to an extent that forces you out of business. When it comes to cost-cutting battles, those with greatest resources inevitably prove to have the upper hand.

Finding the strength and size of the market using market research

Contact with your existing customers can provide a useful guide to what the consumer wants and what he or she is prepared to pay. It should be remembered, however, that their opinions represent no more than those of a small minority.

Desk research

A more objective picture of local or nationwide trends can be gained from performing your own research at your desk. You can start with a row of directories (including Yellow Pages or the phone book) to gauge the size of the market. Your business records represent another valuable starting point for this purpose but in most cases their implications will be limited. Many government departments produce material which can help you to determine the total size of your market and the extent to which it is expanding.

You may find that you can obtain the results of other useful social research by contacting your local Chamber of Commerce or trade association. Enquiries to foreign embassies could also prove productive. Information on overseas markets can often reveal trends that have not yet started in Britain.

Information on your competitors' trading results can be obtained by writing to:

Postal Search Section
Companies Registration Office
Companies House
Crown Way
Cardiff CF4 3UZ

The service will provide details of past trading results for any limited company at a cost of £6.50 per annual set of accounts. A cheque made payable to 'Companies House' should be sent with the orginal letter. The very latest results are unlikely to be available but data from recent years can give valuable clues on sales volumes and underlying costs.

Always remember, however, that any market research you do is of no value unless it is performed with the highest degree of professionalism. Failing to examine information thoroughly could have a severely detrimental effect on your profitability as well as wasting a great deal of your time. *Do Your Own Market Research* by P N Hague and P Jackson (Kogan Page, 1988) is a useful guide to this area.

Market research agencies

An alternative solution to carrying out such tasks yourself is to commission research on your behalf by a specialist market research agency. Many large organisations do this even though they already have their own in-house research departments. There are now some 200 agencies from which to choose. In most cases they sell a wide range of services. Some of these are standard and repeated at regular intervals while others deal with individual problems as they arise. Some of the larger agencies may also specialise in particular aspects of research such as monitoring sales and stocks of consumer goods in the shops.

Obtaining external market research services need not always be prohibitively expensive. Methods such as the omnibus survey, which combines the requirements of a number of individual clients in a single questionnaire, now enable reasonably small-scale operations to obtain essential data at a relatively low cost. The Market Research Society, 15 Northburgh Street, London EC1V OAH (Tel: 071-490 4911) publishes a free directory of organisations that provide market research services. This provides an indication of their size and experience, and a guide, where relevant, to the fields and techniques in which they specialise.

Innovation – keeping on the move

Most successful products are usually the triumph of a winning combination of pricing and performance. Achieving this often involves a certain amount of trial and error. Once it has been attained, however, the process has by no means ended. Every product has a product life cycle, which ends in decline and death. Tastes change rapidly and products can become easily outdated. Indeed, those who hit on the right balance are often among the slowest to innovate and look for new ideas as a result of having become complacent. Make a point of keeping track of fresh moves made by your competitors. Constantly try to think of ways of devising new products and of updating your existing ones, but don't abandon a winning formula just for the sake of change until it shows signs of ageing.

There is no magic formula for inventing a new product. Many profitable ideas in fact result from little more than sudden brainwaves. Nevertheless, those who strive after brainwaves are more likely to have them than those who don't. There is much to be said for setting aside a regular period in which you devote your energies entirely to racking your brains for new ideas. Don't dismiss anything as unrealistic until you have followed it up. Study your own products and those of your competitors. Also encourage suggestions from your staff. Try offering prizes as rewards for good ideas.

Patents

If you feel that you have come up with a novel idea you should try to get it patented. This will give you the right to take legal action against those who attempt to steal it from you. The right can be used to prevent new competition while you develop your idea or to allow another party to exploit your invention and pay you royalties under a licensing agreement. Alternatively, you can sell the patent outright by means of assignment to another person or company.

A UK patent lasts for a maximum period of 20 years from the date on which the application for it is filed. The monopoly protection provided is not enforced automatically. It is the responsibility of the patentee to detect whether his or her rights are being infringed.

Preparing a patent is a highly complex business and will normally require the services of a registered patent agent. For a reasonable consultation fee he or she will be able to visit you at your office and advise you on all aspects of patenting. The way that your application is drawn up will greatly increase your chances of having a patent granted. It will also substantially reduce the chances that your patent will subsequently be revoked. A patent's future validity depends on the fact that what has been stated in its specifications is true.

The agent will arrange a patent search to check that no one has thought of your idea before. The agent may also be able to provide valuable advice concerning the commercial exploitation of your invention. Patent agents are normally listed in Yellow Pages. Alternatively, you could purchase a full list for £2 from:

The Registrar
Chartered Institute of Patent Agents
Staple Inn Buildings
High Holborn
London WC1V 7PZ

To qualify for the grant of a patent an invention must:

1. Be new.
2. Involve an inventive step.
3. Be capable of industrial application.
4. Not be 'excluded'. An invention is not patentable if it is simply a discovery, theory or mental process. Patents will also not be granted to new plant varieties, new methods of medical treatment, or for inventions that could encourage offensive, immoral or anti-social behaviour.

If your invention satisfies these criteria, make sure that you do not publicly disclose it before you have filed your application. Any such disclosures – even those made by word of mouth – could prevent you obtaining a patent or may in due course prove a reason for having it revoked if you do get one.

Details of how to prepare a UK patent application and of the fees involved can be obtained from:

The Patent Office
State House
66–71 High Holborn
London WC1R 4TP
Tel: 071–831 2525

Should you wish to obtain details on how to apply for a European patent you should contact:

The European Patent Office
Erhardtstrasse 27
D–8000 Munchen 2

Points to remember

- Some of the easiest sales are paid for by credit card.
- A shrewd choice of names and symbols can greatly increase your sales.
- People buy for their own reasons and not for yours.
- Establish that there is a market for your products before going any further.
- Try to develop unique selling points.
- Beware of setting prices too low.
- Market research is of no value unless performed thoroughly.
- Make a point of keeping track of your competitors' activities.
- Be constantly thinking of new ideas.
- Unsatisfactory patents can be revoked; use a patent agent.

2
Keeping in Touch with Your Customers

The customer base

Selling to existing customers is invariably very much easier than trying to find new ones. Shopping habits tend to be developed over long periods and are often difficult to break. Most people actually feel happier when dealing with a business they are already familiar with, even if they suspect that they might find a fractionally cheaper price elsewhere. This is because they know that the standard of product, service or advice they are seeking is likely to be acceptable.

Furthermore, a contented customer base should generate a significant proportion of new business through recommendation. Most people are in regular contact with several hundred others during the course of their work and their social lives. When they provide a firm with leads and referrals they often do much of the selling on its behalf.

So your customer base is a vital resource and should be treated as such. It provides you with constant and immediate access to a ready-made market. Detailed records should be maintained of those who have bought from you, and great care should be taken to ensure that these are kept up to date. Do not restrict your records to people's names and addresses alone. Whenever possible try to make a note of their ages, tastes, income brackets and any other information that might give you an insight into their future willingness and ability to buy your products.

There are few more cost-effective methods of increasing your sales than getting existing customers to buy more frequently and in greater quantities than they did previously. Offering direct incentives such as discounts for bulk buying or gift vouchers which can be used towards future purchases of the same goods are methods that are commonly used to this end. Many less obvious and less costly opportunities for maximising the sales potential of the customer base are, however, often ignored.

Keeping in touch

Make every effort to keep in touch with your customers, especially those who have not bought from you for some time. A gentle reminder can work wonders. Make a point also of keeping in touch with those who have not actually bought from you, but who previously expressed an interest in doing so. Contact them at regular intervals. You never know when they might be back in the market again.

The following opportunities for keeping in touch should not be missed:

1. Sending notes of congratulation on the occasion of:
   (a) Birthdays;
   (b) Anniversaries of the date on which a customer opened an account with your business;
   (c) News of recent developments such as a customer being promoted or his firm winning a major new contract.
2. Announcing the launch of new products and services you are providing.
3. Providing details of any special offers you are making such as free gifts, discounts or entry to competitions (see Chapter 5).
4. Announcing changes of address and telephone number or the opening of additional premises.

Product literature

The full potential of your customer base cannot be fully realised unless you are equipped with suitable literature. A well-designed leaflet or catalogue can greatly increase the chances that a customer will extend his interest to other products in your range. It can also provide you with a ready means of selling to leads, referrals and other enquiries you receive or initiate without your having to leave your desk.

There are no fixed rules as to how much a business should spend on its product literature. Those concerns whose range of equipment is very large or highly technical obviously have the greatest need. Whatever your requirements, do not be satisfied with anything less than the highest standards of which you are capable. Product literature is often specifically requested by those who read it. If its contents are of insufficient merit many golden opportunities to increase your sales may be squandered.

Most businesses would be strongly advised to consider having the following:

1. A general leaflet. This should outline your activities and products in broad terms and fit a standard envelope.
2. A comprehensive catalogue. This should provide details of the business's entire product range.
3. A separate sheet for each of the most important products outlining the major features and benefits involved.
4. A price list. This should be kept as simple as possible because it will need to be frequently updated.

The production of effective sales literature is usually the result of sound product knowledge rather than artistic genius. The objective is to explain to the reader in the simplest possible way what he or she will stand to gain from purchasing what you have to offer. Try to use everyday language. Even if your product is highly technical a large proportion of its potential buyers will not share your degree of specialist knowledge.

Establish objectives – how are you going to use the literature?

Sales literature can serve a wide range of functions, so when considering the production of a new leaflet or brochure it is vital that you establish at the outset exactly what you are seeking to achieve. Are you, for example, trying to fulfil an immediate need or aiming to satisfy general requirements? Do you want people to order directly or apply for further information?

The actual method by which you wish people to respond should be thought about seriously. If you operate as a one-man band you may, for example, want to ensure that the bulk of replies are received by post rather than telephone. This will enable you to deal with them in your own time. If, on the other hand, you are trying to encourage people to pay personal visits to a wide range of different outlets, you will have to make provision for including all the necessary addresses.

Initial information

Make a note of all product benefits (for example: lower price, lower running costs, more convenient design, lighter to carry, uses most modern technology) that you wish to stress, together with any general information you intend to include about your company. Gather together ideas for photographs and illustrations and any tables, graphs or other material that you feel you could effectively use. Try to assemble concrete evidence showing that previous customers have been satisfied with what you have to offer. In some cases this could involve producing case studies, such as a letter with a photograph from a 'satisfied customer, Widnes'. Do not, under any circumstances, be tempted to distort the true content of such letters or to invent your own fictional versions.

Seek further advice

Before composing an initial draft of the text consult other members of staff regarding your intended ideas. They might well be able to add a valuable new dimension to your thinking or point to the fact that significant sections of the intended text are not strictly relevant.

Prepare a draft text

Once, and only once, these important initial procedures have been completed should you set about preparing a draft copy of your text. Try to keep your sentences as brief and straightforward as possible. Break up the copy into short segments by using frequent headings and sub-headings. This will help to maintain the reader's interest. At each stage examine the possibility that you have dwelt too long on a particular subject. This is all too easy to do. You are not, after all, restricted in terms of space in the same way as when you are designing press advertisements. But if your catalogue or leaflet is too long it will detract from the chances of its being read from cover to cover and will increase the cost of postage.

Involving other parties

Once you are confident of the approximate length, format and content of your literature you can start to involve the other parties necessary for its completion. You will need to find a suitable designer and printer and possibly even a specialist photographer. Many firms of printers offer design and layout services, but a prerequisite of using these is normally that they do the printing work as well. There is much to be said for keeping the two operations separate.

Printing

Printing costs can vary noticeably from one firm to another and it
is normally a good idea to obtain a handful of different quotations.
Contact with several different printers is also likely to provide you
with a broad range of informal advice on whether your initial
selections of size and format can be altered to achieve greater cost
effectiveness. The costs of printing and paper have been rising
rapidly and every effort should be made to seek a keen quotation.
Nevertheless, do not be tempted by cheap estimates which imply
the use of poor grades of paper. The quality of paper that is used
is a highly important factor in conveying the desired image of your
firm. Be wary also of attractive discounts that you are offered for
exceptionally large print runs. Put them in their true perspective.
Sales literature can go out of date very quickly. It is often wise to
avoid the temptation to save a few pounds if it involves the risk of
wasting many hundreds.

If you are seeking quotations from printers with whom you are
not familiar make sure they provide an efficient delivery service
and that the cost of this is covered in their original estimate. To
have to leave your desk for the purposes of collection would
constitute a quite unnecessary burden.

Designers

There is much to be said for choosing one designer to assist with
all your affairs – including your advertising – and to stick with him
or her. To achieve an effective working relationship in the first
place will take time. He or she must become fully conversant with
the workings of your business. This will involve frequent visits to
your office. They may also be able to adapt or reuse material from
previous campaigns. This should save you money as freelance
designers tend to charge for their services at an hourly rate rather
than on a fixed fee basis for a particular project.

Selecting the right designer in the first place can prove time-
consuming, but the effort involved is strictly necessary. Seek
recommendations from friends and colleagues. Should no suitable
leads be forthcoming try answering enquiries from advertisements
in trade magazines or telephoning some of the entries listed under
'Artists' or 'Designers' in Yellow Pages or your Thomson Local
Directory. Briefly discuss your objectives and draw up a shortlist
of potentially suitable candidates. Invite these for face-to-face
talks.

Ensure liaison between designer and printer

Remember that you are dealing with specialists and that some areas of their duties are not easily understandable. You should thus be wary of talking at cross-purposes with different parties. Insist that your designer contact your printer on your behalf to check that his or her intended designs match those that the printer was expecting and to establish the format in which they must be presented if they are to be reproduced. Be sure that the colours chosen are to your liking. In general, bold reds and oranges sell better than insipid greens and blues.

Photographs

You should make as much use of colour photographs in a catalogue as possible. They will go a long way towards compensating for the fact that you will not be leaving your desk to make a sales presentation. Unless you or any of your staff are extremely capable in what is a highly complicated field you should get your photographs commissioned professionally. Many of the secrets of the art of good photography are not immediately obvious to the uninitiated.

Make sure that any photographs appearing on the cover of your catalogue refer to your leading products, otherwise you have wasted a valuable opportunity. You might well find that your designer is able to offer you useful advice on photographic matters. But remember that use of extra colour can add greatly to the cost of printing, especially on short runs.

Checking

There are few worse advertisements for a company than sales literature which is full of errors. When mistakes occur they all too often involve important and prominent details because the person concerned has taken for granted the fact that these must be correct. Checking processes tend to centre around those minor points where the margin for error is perceived to be greatest. Thus, however many times you have checked the final version of your literature, make sure that someone else gives it a thorough examination before it actually goes to print.

Points to remember

- Selling to existing customers is usually easier than finding new ones.

- Make every effort to keep in touch with existing customers.
- Keep the language of all sales literature simple.
- There is much to be said for using one designer for all your affairs.
- There are few worse advertisements than sales literature full of errors.

3
Using the Post

The postal service is a formidable sales weapon. It provides you with access to every business and household in the country without having to leave your desk. Selling through the post – or by 'direct mail' as the medium is most commonly known – was the fastest growing means of marketing in the UK during the 1980s and is still growing. In many major firms the method now forms an accepted and essential component of the overall marketing mix.

Direct mail: expensive but very effective

Direct mail is, in fact, one of the more expensive forms of selling in terms of cost per number of people actually reached. But, if used with skill and planning, it is among the most accurate with regard to locating the required target audience and can therefore be highly cost-effective.

The difference between ordinary advertising and direct mail is like the difference between an old-fashioned musket pumping out grapeshot and a deadly, modern high velocity rifle used by a skilled assassin. It can hit the chosen target much more often.

Advantages for the customer

Direct mail makes life easier for the customer. The advantages are:

1. Little effort or sacrifice is necessary from the buyer, and customers who live in remote areas or who are housebound can be contacted.
2. Some folk are shy of sales people by nature. Others prefer the confidentiality of dealing through the post or like to peruse information in their own time rather than under the pressure of a face-to-face appointment.
3. Information in writing can normally be conveyed with greater

clarity than by word of mouth, and space in a letter is decidedly less limited than is the case with press advertising.

4. A much more personal approach can be taken.
5. Some people assume that they are automatically getting a keener price when buying through the post than when using more routine outlets.

Direct mail is an easily quantifiable medium – the results can be measured. By monitoring your response rates you can establish with accuracy the cost-effectiveness of any campaign. And you can see whether you will be wasting your money before you spend too much of it! Exploratory tests carried out to determine the strength of your sales pitch are relatively straightforward. You simply send out, say, 1000 shots and see how they work before you send out 5000 or 10,000 or 100,000. Mailings can be carried out in any quantities you choose, large or small, and therefore are not beyond the reach of those operating on slender budgets. A very small business with limited resources can sell through the post, even if this entails restricting its approaches to a mere handful of established customers.

The publisher of this book started his company by direct mail, selling a book from his kitchen table. He now runs a £4 million publishing firm, with sales all over the world.

The importance of targeting

A mailing campaign will never be successful unless it is directed at the right audience. This fact cannot be over-emphasised. A shoddy mailing that is effectively targeted will almost certainly produce better results than an exceptional one sent to the wrong people. So you must go to a lot of trouble to locate suitable prospects. This will never be achieved cost-effectively by despatching letters in vast indiscriminate volumes.

Lists are king (or queen)

Your mailing lists, once proved, will be your most cherished marketing possession. You should soon learn, after using the list a number of times, which of your main targets will buy and in what quantities. As discussed in Chapter 2, your most productive target area will be your bank of existing customers, and those who have bought from you most often and most recently are likely to provide the best returns.

Business people venturing outside their own client base have two principal alternatives available to them. They can either compile their own lists of likely prospects or they can rent mailing lists from other organisations. Those who draw up their own lists are likely to achieve better results than if they rent from others. Their target area will have been specifically selected to match the requirements of the product being marketed. Gathering the necessary material can, however, prove time-consuming. The individual concerned must try to conjure up a picture of the ideal prospect for the goods or services being sold. He or she must determine at which social classes, age groups, income brackets or geographical areas they are being aimed.

Finding suitable lists

Apart from your own customer list, trade and industry year-books, directories and registers are among those items that can be effectively employed without leaving your desk. It may also be worth phoning appropriate trade associations or Chambers of Commerce to enquire whether they have any relevant literature available. Always remember that a source giving the actual name of the person you wish to contact is more valuable than one which merely provides an address. Be wary of collecting information that might be out of date. One in five of any list of named persons will, on average, move, change jobs, die or retire in a year.

Sometimes suitable mailing lists can be rented from publishing houses and similar organisations which have built up a substantial database for the purposes of their own trade. But the most comprehensive lists are obtained from the numerous list brokers who loan you a list from a vast range of target areas. The lists they have available cater for a broad range of requirements and additional ones can be conjured up, tailored to order. But they will need to know the purpose behind your mailing and this may well involve asking to see a sample of the product you are selling. The average charge made for renting a mailing list is in the region of £70 per 1000 names, but it can be more or less than that. In general, you get what you pay for – often an expensive, exclusive and highly targeted list is well worth the extra cost.

Several reference works are in circulation which provide a guide to available lists. These are *Benn's Direct Marketing Services* (£75, Benn's Business Information Services Limited), *Lists and Data Sources* (£80, Ladson House Publishers), *BRAD Direct Marketing List Rates and Data* (£95, Maclean Hunter Ltd) and *The Direct*

Mail Databook (£49.50, Gower). Useful additional information may also come to light through contacting the Direct Mail Producers Association (081-883 9854) and the British Direct Marketing Association (071-630 7322).

The mailing industry has three magazines which can help to ensure that you keep up to date with any new lists that become available and other news relevant to your activities. *Precision Marketing* (Centaur Communications – £40 per annum) is issued weekly, while *Direct Marketing International* (Charterhouse Communications – subscription free upon request) and *Direct Response Magazine* (Direct Response Magazine Ltd – £45 per annum) are issued monthly. There is much to be said for subscribing to at least one of these.

Prune those lists!

Just as it is vital to locate the right people to mail-shot it is also important to avoid the wrong ones. If you receive requests from people asking to be removed from your mailing lists you should take notice of them. Failure to do so is not only irresponsible, it is also wasting your time and money. Sending a mailing to that person in future makes as much commercial sense as throwing money down the drain.

If you are indulging in mailings in any significant volume it could well prove worthwhile to subscribe to the Mailing Preference Service (MPS). This is a non-profit making organisation which offers consumers the facility to have their names and home addresses excluded from or added to mailing lists controlled or used by its members – who account for over 80 per cent of mailing campaigns that take place in this country. Details of those consumers who have contacted the service are recorded on a tape which is sent at quarterly intervals to members who pay for the privilege by subscription. For those mailing in volumes of under half a million letters a year membership costs £400 per annum. The number of consumers registered with the MPS had already reached 250,000 in 1990 and is increasing rapidly. The service can be contacted by writing to:

Mailing Preference Service
1 Leeward House
Plantation Wharf
London SW11 3TY

You will invariably get some of your letters returned marked 'gone away'. Don't forget to delete those names from your lists and return the envelopes to the agency you rented them from, for rebate. It will stop you wasting money the next time you use that mailing list.

Mail-shot content and presentation

However accurately you have targeted your audience, it should be remembered that you will not be the first person to send them a mail-shot. Most households have now come to accept the receipt of unsolicited mail as a fact of life, so your task in capturing the recipient's attention is not an easy one. You have only a matter of seconds in which to arouse interest.

If people are to be persuaded to part with money they must be convinced that the organisation they are dealing with is well established and highly professional in approach. In most cases your mailing will be the only thing they have to go on. The type of paper that you use is particularly important in conveying the right impression. Always go for quality rather than quantity. See-through or other poor grades of paper will undoubtedly have an adverse effect on response rates.

Exactly what you enclose in your mailing package will depend on the type of product you are seeking to sell and the budget you have available. Sometimes a letter on its own will suffice. In other circumstances a clear case can be made for including additional items. If, for example, you are selling a straightforward low-cost but high-volume product – such as polythene bags or toilet paper – it may well pay to enclose a sample. There is, however, no actual guarantee that a very expensive mailing will outperform a cheap one. Indeed, the reverse is often the case. If you are promoting a range of products you may decide to include a catalogue or pamphlet. All these imponderables can be settled by doing trial mailings before sending out large quantities of expensive brochures or samples.

How to increase response rates

You should always try to include some method of prompting interested parties into action. Admiration on its own will not make you any money. It is sales that you are after. Some prospects may be very keen on what you have to offer but may not get around to placing an order because they are lazy or disorganised. Others may want to postpone coming to a decision for the immediate future. The easier you make it for people to buy from you and the more pressure you put on them to do so, the greater your chances of increasing your sales. Do not be afraid to point out what the prospect may have to lose by not buying. Stating a limited supply or a fixed period within which a reply must be received can greatly improve response levels. So also can including a local telephone number on which you may be contacted or a separate order form with a reply-paid facility. An incentive like a discount or free gift for early ordering can be very effective.

An application form for a licence to have your own reply-paid cards and envelopes can be obtained from the Customer Care Unit at your local Post Office head office. The cost of such a licence is £27.50 a year. You will be charged in addition for every reply-paid item returned to you through the post at a rate of ½ pence above the current rates for first- and second-class mail delivered in the UK. Such payments are made through an account which you open with the Post Office. Money in advance will be required from you for the purpose. The amount requested varies from one area of the country to another but is normally in the region of £50. Your account is then debited on a weekly basis. Once its balance descends to around £10 you will receive an invoice requesting a top-up.

Try to provide a credit card facility (see Chapter 1). Don't be afraid to include incentives but make sure they are easy to understand and serious in nature. Avoid hilarious gimmicks and novelties. Being outrageously unusual can be great fun but rarely proves sound commercial practice. The average British citizen likes special offers but is essentially conservative in taste and outlook. You can buy a vast range of incentives – card wallets, cheap watches, calculators and so on from a number of specialist suppliers.

The envelope

Your envelope is more than just a container. It is the first part of your mailing package that the recipient will see. Indeed, in theory, if it creates a highly unfavourable impression it could be the only part. In practice, however, most people open virtually all the envelopes they receive. The are too curious and greedy not to do so. But a well-presented envelope will do more than just ensure that it is opened. It will whet the appetite of the person concerned and increase the chances of due attention being paid to the enclosed material.

Your envelopes should match the quality of the paper they contain. They should be properly sealed and their contents should be suitably folded. Stamps should be mounted squarely in the top right-hand corner. Pay scrupulous attention to the accuracy of the prospect's name and address and avoid using stick-on labels. Full postcodes should be used if available. Specific titles people use before their names and letters after them should always be included. In most cases the owners have worked hard to achieve them and are thus very proud of them. When no such titles are in evidence names should be prefixed with Mr, Mrs, Miss or Ms. It is normally fairly easy to work out whether a prospect is male or female. Trying to determine whether a lady is married or single can, however, present problems. If you are unsure always address her as Ms. Never guess.

All your envelopes should carry your own address on the outside so that the Post Office can return them to you if their destination turns out to be incorrect. This will help to ensure that your mailing list is kept accurate and up to date. The nature of your campaign will play a major part in determining whether any further wording or visual effects should be included. In some circumstances a case can be made for adding a special message or involvement device to capture the prospect's attention. If you are mailing your existing customers, however, or if you have a particularly striking company logo this should not be necessary.

The letter

When people open an envelope they expect to find a letter inside. So however many items you include, make sure that your letter is the first thing they see. If you are trying to cut back on the contents of your mailing package never sacrifice your letter. Its presence is essential. Do without something else instead.

Long letters are invariably more effective than short ones. Nevertheless, make sure that you don't include excessive detail for its own sake. Your writing style must be pertinent and factual. When composing your letter remember the simple magic formula: AIDA. The letters stand for Attention, Interest, Desire, Action. If you can arouse these qualities in your reader in this order you are well on the way to writing the perfect sales letter.

In order to command your prospect's attention your opening should be both personal and dramatic. Ideally, it should stress a benefit that he or she is guaranteed to realise if your offer is taken up. Then expand on the advantages of what you are selling. Try to ensure that you qualify your enthusiasm with concrete proof and examples. Say why you are better than your competitors and stress any fringe benefits that you may have available, such as a guarantee or a back-up service. End with a summary of all the major selling points you have mentioned.

The layout of your letter is just as important as its content. It must look attractive and easy to read. Keep your paragraphs brief and begin them with large indents. Use wide margins on both sides of the page and keep your lines short – not longer than 10 words on average. Increase the width of your margin for paragraphs that need particular emphasis. If you feel the urge to indulge in any underlining make sure that you restrict this to key points. Excessive use of highlighting techniques will make the copy difficult to read and cast aspersions on your ability to communicate.

The exact contents of your letter will, of course, depend on what you are selling and who you are trying to persuade to buy. No one letter will thus suit everyone's needs. But a study of the example on page 35 provides a valuable guide to many of the considerations involved. The letter has been used with great effect by Wyvern Business Library, which sells business books by mail order.

Never photocopy your letters. If you do so people will always notice that their names and addresses have been entered in a different grade of type. Much of the personal approach which you are depending on for your success will then have been lost. If you are dealing in reasonably small quantities you should use a word processor. Do not forget to ensure that you sign each letter personally. If you are considering mailing in heavy volumes it may be worth employing a direct marketing agency to perform the task on your behalf (see Chapter 7).

Perhaps the most important part of the letter is the postscript – it's almost always read, so make good use of it. You can use it to re-emphasise the attractions of what you are offering, or to hammer home your incentive offer, or to sell the customer some additional item.

The order form

You should always include a carefully designed order form in your mail-shot – either on your leaflet or your letter or separately. You must make it easy to place an order with you. So give enough room for the customer's name and address, a credit card number and a box to tick for the selection. And always code the form so you know which list produced the order. An example which you can adapt is shown on page 37.

Practical books for business

How to use the law to get money owed to you

CASH COLLECTION *Action Kit*

A complete guide to recovering money by arbitration proceedings in the County Court

PHILIP CEGAN and JANE HARRISON

Dear Business Manager,

When all your credit control systems are exhausted and you STILL haven't been paid – what should you do?

This book starts where most credit control books stop. It is the complete guide to taking legal action in the small claims court (and enforcing the judgement) to recover money owed to you.*

Hardened debtors expect you to run out of steam

Reminder letters, final demands, collection agencies, solicitors' letters, then court proceedings – you begin to wonder whether the debt is worth the effort. Hardened debtors (and usually the ones who owe the most) rely on that.

But if you know exactly what to do when, have all the relevant documents prepared and waiting, know your options in advance and follow through systematically – most of the effort is taken out of the problem.

Everything you need to knock them out in court

This book contains examples of all the documents you are likely to need, detailed descriptions of what to do when, and full information about what costs and expenses are recoverable.

And if your claim is straightforward, then you are unlikely even to need to consult a solicitor.

How to enforce a judgement

But this book doesn't just stop there. Here you will find everything you need to know to ENFORCE a judgement.

If the court decides in your favour (and it is bound to if you are in the right and followed the instructions in this book) it is still possible for the debtor to choose to ignore the

Readymade letters and legal forms to follow a case through the couts and enforce judgement.

Contents

1 Arbitration and the County Court

2 Collecting Payment without Suing

3 Starting Litigation

The letter before action
Offer of payment by the debtor
Commencement of proceedings

4 Defended Actions

5 The Arbitration Hearing

6 Enforcing Your Judgement

Examination of means
Warrant of execution
Attachment of earnings
Garnishee proceedings
Charging order

Glossary

Appendices

1 Draft agreement for the Supply of Goods and/or Services (non-commercial)
2 Schedule of Court Fees, Fixed Costs and Other Fees Payable in Connection with County Court Proceedings

Index

* Normal arbitration maximum is £500 although sums up to £5,000 can be dealt with. Your case must be suitable for arbitration in a county court in England and Wales.

P.T.O.

judgement. And the court won't do anything about it unless you require it to do so. Don't give up now. You are very close to getting your money.

Chapter 6 – Enforcing Your Judgement – gives you five methods of enforcement.

Examination of means, for example, gives you the opportunity to cross-examine the debtor in court on his assets. But you can ask very wide ranging questions (12 suggested ones are given). This often panics the debtor into telling the truth and making an offer (which the court can enforce using a garnishee - instructions to the debtor's bank to pay the money directly over to you).

Warrants of execution, attachments of earnings, garnishee proceedings and charging orders are all powerful legal ways to get debts paid.

When they know what you can do, they often pay up

You will frequently find that debtors don't realise just how far you can go to get your money. And many don't believe you will have the stamina to follow through. A change of heart is remarkably common when they learn the facts and witness your resolve. Most pay up without further ado.

With this slim but powerful book in your credit control armoury, no debtor should get away with it ever again.

Yours sincerely,

[signature]

Michael Herbert
Managing Director

P.S. In my experience, once your credit control system has failed to collect a debt and court action has been threatened, you get best results by moving as rapidly as possible. Nothing is more unnerving for the debtor trying to get away without paying (ie. stealing from you). This book tells you everything you need to know NOW — so you are fully prepared in advance.

=== Wyvern ===
Business *[Wyvern logo]* **Library**   *Practical books for business*

A Wyvern Group Company

Wyvern House, 6 The Business Park, Ely, Cambs CB7 4JW. ☎ Ely (0353) 665544 (Fax: 0353 667666)

General Manager: J.D. Rutherford BA A division of Wyvern Crest Limited. Registered Office as above. Registered in England No. 1496358. Registered under the Data Protection Act. VAT No. 432 1941 74. Directors: M.C. Herbert MA MSc (Managing) A.B. Fanning BA, I.B.F. Fanning BA, D.S. Roche BD MRSH MITD, S.M. Herbert (Secretary)

Order Form

Complete this form and
return with payment to:
Freepost (*If you use it;
followed by your name and
address*)
or telephone your order and
credit card details now on
(*your telephone number*)
Fax your order on (*your fax
number*)

Please send me _____
(*Itemise goods on offer*)

I enclose a cheque for £___
payable to (*your name*)
(please add (?) p&p).

Card details: Access/Visa/
Amex/DC number:

☐☐☐☐☐☐☐☐☐☐☐☐☐☐☐☐

Expires _____

Name on card: _____

Please type or print clearly:

Name _____

Position _____

Company/Institution _____

Address _____

_____

_____

Postcode _____

Signature _____

Date _____
(*Code for responses*)

**Kogan Page Money Back
Guarantee.
If you are not satisfied with
your purchase, return it to us
in saleable condition within
14 days and we will refund
your money immediately.**

Testing the market

Never indulge in any mass mailings until you have tested both
your mailing package and your mailing list in small quantities. Do
not draw any conclusions until you have mailed the same people
on at least two, and preferably three, occasions. Like other forms
of advertising, direct mail requires a degree of repetition to be fully
effective. Vary the approach that you make on each separate
occasion. This will give you the opportunity to sell your product
from different angles and to find out which method of presentation
is most effective. Experiment with different incentives and

designs. If you are using a pamphlet or brochure it may be a good idea to test the merits of colour against those of black and white.

But once you have hit on a winning formula, stick to it. Even when you have grown tired of the same old leaflet, do not discard it until you have real evidence that something else works better for you. It should be relatively easy to determine what each reply and each sale have cost to produce. The response rate you require to make a profit will obviously depend to a large extent on the cost of the mailing and the basic profit margins involved with the products you are promoting. By means of the same simple arithmetic calculations described you should have little difficulty in working out the response you need to achieve to break even. A 2 per cent response has traditionally been regarded as a respectable rate of return. Many companies even operate profitably on a rate of only ½ per cent. This is because the basic profit margins involved with the goods and services they are selling are extremely large. If you achieve a response rate nearing 10 per cent and operate on a reasonable profit margin you can rest assured that you are on to a winner.

If you have a response rate of, say, 2 per cent, it means that you must send out 50 mail shots to make a single sale. If costs, with postage, addressing, list rental, printing and inserting etc, amount to 40p per envelope, to obtain a sale on a 2 per cent response costs you:

$$50 \times 40p = £20$$

To that you must add the cost of your product and overheads, so the price of the product must be well over £20 to make a profit. But that is not the end of the story.

First, with a well designed and well aimed shot, you might get a better response than 2 per cent. Doubling the response to 4 per cent means halving your break-even amount. And then, having got the names and addresses of those who have responded, you will have a list for your next mailing that will achieve much higher responses and profits in future. Many book clubs, for example, lose money on their first campaigns but speedily turn in good profits on later campaigns because of their enriched mailing lists, containing known, named customers who are likely to order.

If you achieve a high, profitable response rate on a list, try it again, removing the names that have already responded. You are likely to get a further, worthwhile response.

Increasing the volume

Once you know that your mailing formats are effective and that your lists represent a suitable target area you can proceed to step up the volume of your activities. Avoid times such as the Christmas period or the peak of the holiday season. Keep accurate records. One solution is to have two separate series of index cards: one for prospects who you intend to mail – or who you have mailed but have not as yet replied – and the other for customers who have bought from you already. Record here details of each mailing, response and sale that occurs. Make the appropriate transfers and deletions between one series and the other. If your business begins to grow in a big way, you will, of course, have to consider using a computer to record these details.

The postal service

The Royal Mail aims to deliver (Monday to Saturday in the UK) first-class letters the day after collection and most second-class letters the third working day after collection. In practice a substantial proportion of deliveries do not meet these schedules. However, our postal service compares favourably with those of other countries. Indeed, research suggests that it is the cheapest and most cost-effective in Europe. Rises in UK postal charges have been notably modest. During the last five years they have risen by around 7 per cent below the rate of inflation while the costs of TV and press advertising have grown at a rate of between 20 to 30 per cent above that of inflation.

The special facilities available for the business user are particularly impressive. There is no need for you to leave your desk to post your mail. You can arrange for the Post Office to collect it for you. If you require mail to be collected five days a week on a regular basis the annual charge is £300. For regular collections at less frequent intervals the charge reduces directly in proportion to the number of days a week involved. So if you need mail collected once a week, it will cost you £60 a year. The service can be applied for by contacting the Collection Duty Department at the Customer Care Unit at your local Post Office head office. The department can also arrange for mail to be collected from you on an irregular basis but requires 24 hours' notice for the purpose. The charge for a one-off collection of this nature is £2.10. If 1000 or more letters are involved, however, it is free.

Until recently there were a number of different schemes available to business people seeking preferential rates on their mailings. Now there is only one known as Mailsort. It enables business users who are mailing in volumes of over 4000 letters or 1000 packets to obtain discounts in return for carrying out some of the sorting work that would otherwise be undertaken by the Royal Mail. Collection is free.

It offers three different delivery options providing a choice between speed and economy. These are:

Mailsort 1: first class, target delivery next working day.

Mailsort 2: second class, target delivery within three working days.

Mailsort 3: economy class, target delivery within seven working days.

With Mailsort 1 you could save up to 15 per cent of your postage costs. Maximum savings on Mailsort 2 are 13 per cent and with Mailsort 3 they can be between 25 and 32 per cent. The use of the postcode is essential to the service and is the key to obtaining its higher discounts.

Since January 1991 at least 85 per cent of Mailsort mail has had to be fully postcoded – with at least a further 5 per cent with the outward code. Royal Mail account managers, available to assist you with getting Mailsort up and running in your company, can be contacted via the Customer Care Unit at your local Post Office head office.

Points to remember

- Mailings will only be cost-effective if aimed at the right audience; don't economise (either with time or money) on getting the right mailing list.
- Never mail in large volumes unless you have tested the market.
- Keep accurate records
- You have only a matter of seconds in which to interest your prospect.
- Go for quality rather than quantity when selecting your paper.
- Design your order form with care to make it easy for the purchaser to respond and to give you maximum information about him/herself for future use, and remember to code it.
- Always include a letter, and don't forget to use the postscript.

- Never photocopy your letters.
- Always include your own business address on the envelope.
- Mailsort is available for high-volume fully postcoded mail.
- It is not necessary to leave your desk to post your mail.
- Keep careful records of expenditure and revenue, and work out your break-even point.
- Repeat mailings on profitable lists.

4
Using the Telephone

The last few years have seen a marked increase in the use of the telephone as a sales and marketing tool, both as a means of approach and as a method of response. The boom is far from over. The telephone can be employed to great effect at virtually every stage of the selling cycle. It can be used to generate response from advertising, conduct market research, build customer loyalty, arrange face-to-face appointments for sales people, or even sell directly. It can be used both as an isolated weapon and in conjunction with other marketing devices. The practice of securing orders over the phone is known as 'telesales'. Virtually every other telephone dialogue that contributes to a sale falls into the category 'telemarketing'.

Incoming calls

The telephone enables the staff of a business to speak directly with customers from the comfort of their own premises and working atmosphere. In the case of incoming calls, however, this privilege can prove to be a disadvantage to those who fail to exploit it efficiently. Callers do not phone within prescribed time limits, but at their own convenience. They are thus often capable of catching a firm unawares.

This must always be borne in mind when deciding whether or not to provide the option replying by telephone to an advertising campaign. Letters received through the post can, to a certain extent, be processed by an advertiser in his or her own time. When the phone rings, however, it must be answered within a matter of seconds. A reply by telephone that is dealt with correctly will almost certainly create a more favourable impression than the impersonal sending of information through the post. On those occasions when callers do not receive due consideration, however, business may well be lost. It is therefore essential that all members of staff are fully conversant with telephone techniques. The person who answers the phone will in many cases be providing a caller with the first impression of a company. An important phone call from someone intending to place thousands of pounds' worth of business could well arrive when all but one of a department are out to lunch.

For the sole trader with a single phone line the problem of not being able to predict when people are going to phone is invariably felt even more deeply. If he or she is not present the answerphone must be relied on. It is surprising, however, how many callers fail to leave messages on answerphones. Often they are put off by the length of the recorded announcement. The secret is to keep the recording brief. Tell the caller who you are, apologise for not being available and invite the leaving of name and number. Avoid other unnecessary details.

Even when a sole trader is in the office there is the problem that the line is often engaged. If callers cannot get through their curiosity may wane and further attempts may not be made. One way of reducing this problem is to take advantage of British Telecom's Call Waiting Service. (This is available only to those with digitalised lines.) If a business line is constantly busy the service can prevent important calls being missed. A special beeping tone indicates when a third party is trying to make contact during an existing telephone conversation. The original conversation can be put on hold while the identity of the new caller is determined. There is no connection charge for the Call Waiting Service although there is a rental cost of £3.48 per quarter. Those seeking to apply for the service should phone the operator on 100 and ask to be put in touch with the British Telecom Business Sales Department for their area.

The following points should be borne in mind for incoming calls received both in the course of routine business and as a direct result of advertising.

1. Treat each and every telephone call you receive with the same respect and importance as those that you make. Callers may not be seeking to place orders, but if dealt with effectively they may well do so on a subsequent occasion. If you phone a potential customer who does not want to buy you have merely exhausted one of several thousand, or even million, potential leads. If, however, you fail to deal with an existing customer

satisfactorily you have almost certainly squandered the opportunity to obtain easy future business.

2. Put as much of your telephone conversations as possible in writing. Keep note pads by the phone.

3. Always speak clearly and do not be afraid to repeat facts that you feel may not have been understood.

4. The recipient of the call should always begin the conversation by stating the name of the department and company that has been contacted.

5. Impeccable standards of politeness should be adhered to. Never shout or be off-hand. Always listen to complaints sympathetically. Remember that any customer who has contacted you to express dissatisfaction is in effect providing you with a valuable opportunity to rectify the situation.

6. Avoid irrelevancies. Although you will always get the odd person who likes a chat, the majority of callers will be seeking to have their needs fulfilled in as short a time as possible.

7. Always end with a brief summary of the main points of the conversation. This will help to ensure that you have not been talking at cross purposes and increase the chances that your discussion will be remembered.

8. Make sure that all records are within easy reach of the phone. If your record-keeping has been methodical you will be able to summon details of a customer's previous correspondence and orders within only a matter of seconds of the call being answered.

Special response numbers

Those seeking to maximise their response from advertisements would be well advised to consider looking beyond merely using their own standard phone number. Several methods are commonly exploited as marketing tools.

0800 numbers

The presence of a Linkline 0800 number enables a business to be telephoned free of charge. The bill is footed by the company rather than the caller. This can do much to increase loyalty from existing customers and greatly encourage first-time enquirers. Calls can be made from anywhere in the UK (an international service is also available). Calls are delivered over a special network and a company can receive these on an ordinary phone, a switchboard or automatic call distribution system.

The cost of running such a service is:

Connection charge of £250 per line.
Plus quarterly rental of £100 per line.
Plus call charges as follows:
16 pence a minute peak rate – 9am to 1pm Monday to Friday.
12 pence a minute standard rate – 1pm to 6pm Monday to Friday.
9 pence a minute cheap rate – 6pm to 9am and weekends.

The service can be applied for by telephoning 0800 333 222. You will be asked for some brief details and then given the number of a local consultant to contact.

0345 numbers

Linkline 0345 numbers operate on broadly the same lines as 0800 numbers. The difference lies in the fact that the cost of the call is split between the caller and the company. The caller can phone in from anywhere in the UK but is charged at his local rate only. The company pays for the rest.

The cost of running such a service is:

Connection charge £250 per line.
Plus quarterly rental of £100 per line.
Plus call charges as follows:
13 pence a minute peak rate – 9am to 1pm Monday to Friday.
10 pence a minute standard rate – 1pm to 6pm Monday to Friday.
9 pence a minute cheap rate – 6pm to 9am and weekends.

The service can also be applied for by telephoning 0800 333 222.

Freefone

As with 0800 numbers a Freefone service enables a caller to contact a business free of charge. Here the call is made through the operator with the caller requesting the company's personal identifying Freefone name. The operator logs all calls, including details of their origins, and this information is in due course passed to the company concerned. The service thus provides an extremely useful market research function as the sources from which business is generated can be easily identified.

Freefone is particularly useful in those forms of advertising, such as radio, where the prospect has only a limited chance of remembering a telephone number. The likelihood of someone recalling a number such as 0800 534 391 on the first occasion it is heard is limited unless it is written down. If told to phone 'Freefone Skyland', however, the caller is more likely to remember the necessary details.

The costs of the service up to 31 March 1991 are:

> Set-up charge £250 for national coverage, or £50 for local coverage per British Telecom district. (Those who pay for five districts have an automatic right to national coverage should they require it.)
> Plus quarterly rental of £20.
> Plus call charges of 25 pence per call added to standard British Telecom operator rates.

The service can be applied for by dialling the operator and asking for 'Freefone Assistance'. The caller will then be sent an application form for completion.

Premium rate

A premium rate service offers an advertiser the opportunity to obtain additional revenue by charging callers at a rate above the normal standard one. The main premium rate service is operated by British Telecom. This issues phone numbers prefixed with 0898. Other rival services have also been launched by Mercury (0839) and Racal Vodafone (0836). A caller dialling an 0898 number will be charged at 33 pence a minute at the cheap rate (6pm to 8am Monday to Friday, weekends and Bank Holidays) or at 44 pence a minute at all other times.

Such lines can be used with great effect to enable callers to listen to pre-recorded material or to leave their own brief messages. In the latter capacity the lines can prove particularly suitable for assisting with competitions and quizzes. In some cases voice recognition equipment, which enables the caller to conduct a conversation with a computer, is available.

The equipment needed to stage an 0898 reply service is sufficiently bulky and costly to preclude outright purchase as a viable proposition to the smaller business person. There are two alternatives. Apply to have a line managed by British Telecom – details of this service can be obtained by dialling 0800 800 898 and requesting an 0898 Callstream brochure. Alternatively, approach an independent company which leases lines from a premium rate supplier. Broadsystem, TIS, Legion and Cablecom have all established a presence in the market-place. British Telecom pays them 22½ pence a minute for calls received. The proportion of this sum actually refunded to clients will vary from one case to another. Most are likely to be open to negotiation.

Outgoing calls

Outgoing telesales and telemarketing calls can perform a wide variety of functions. The following considerations, however, apply almost universally.

Different purposes

Don't be afraid to put calls to more than one purpose. If, for example, you are making a sales call to a prospect who does not want to buy, you may find that he or she is still interested in receiving your catalogue. You may also find that you are able to obtain valuable market research information. Even if you fail to achieve anything concrete your phone call should still have served as a valuable PR exercise. In the same way that press coverage and advertising can whet appetites, your professionalism and manner should be such that a prospect's interest will be aroused on the next occasion when he or she comes across your organisation. Under no circumstances, however, should you attempt to make sales calls in the guise of market research. The practice is highly unethical and specifically disapproved of by the Office of Fair Trading. The basic purpose of any phone call – together with the caller's and company's name – should be made abundantly clear at the beginning of every conversation.

Cost

Effective use of the telephone can prove highly cost-effective. But as the phone is one of the most expensive methods by which potential sources of new business can be contacted, every opportunity should be taken to minimise the amount of unnecessary time spent on calls.

Simplicity

Avoid complex conversations. If the product or idea concerned is highly technical the telephone is not the right medium through which to promote it.

Test different approaches

The telephone offers you the opportunity to test different approaches with far greater ease than most other sales and marketing tools. One script can be substituted for another in a matter of minutes. Telemarketers should always be on the lookout for ways of improving their techniques and constantly experimenting with different formats.

A numbers game

The more calls made, the greater are the chances of obtaining the results being sought. The need for organisation is paramount. Those who waste one minute between every phone call will talk to far fewer decision-makers every working day than those who do not. Specific targets should be set for the number of calls intended to be made in any one day. Keep accurate records of your results. When the person you are trying to contact is at a meeting, be sure to make a note of when he or she will be available. Constant phone calls can be tedious, so a positive attitude is essential. Do not allow the element of repetition to get you down. It is vital that you sound enthusiastic on every call you make.

Finding suitable prospects

Do not compose your own telephone numbers at random. The practice is unlikely to prove cost-effective. You will have no idea whether you are telephoning a business or a household. In some cases you will dial numbers that don't actually exist. The practice is also unethical. Those who register as ex-directory do so for a reason.

Many of the targeting considerations and sources for finding prospects are the same as those involved when using the post – see Chapter 3. Not all mailing lists, however, contain phone numbers. If you are dealing with a list broker it is essential to establish that you are seeking lists which can be used for telemarketing or telesales purposes.

Timing of calls

Finding the right people to telephone is one thing. Approaching them at the right time can prove equally important. The more occasions on which you are able to make direct contact with a prospect, the more profitable your day's calling will be. Similarly, by catching a decision-maker at a convenient time there is a greater chance that he or she will cooperate to your satisfaction.

Phoning at lunchtime should be avoided in the case of the majority of business-to-business calls. Even in hotels and restaurants, where decision-makers are almost certain to be in,

Telephone record form

Prospect name _____

Position _____

Company/Institution _____

Department _____

Address _____

_____

_____ Postcode _____

Phone no _____

Best time to call_____

Size of business (no of branches/employees/£)_____

Type of business_____

Prospect needs _____

Product or service to offer_____

Features to emphasise_____

Decision-maker's name_____

Date	Result	Follow-up if any

Sales history

they will probably be too busy to grant you the level of attention you desire. Some business people are more likely to be available at certain hours than others. Builders, carpenters and plumbers, for example, are most likely to be phoned back with greatest effect either first thing in the morning before they have gone out to work or in the early evening after they have returned.

Attempts to contact domestic prospects are most effectively made either in the evenings or at weekends. Phone rates are at their cheapest and calls are much more likely to be answered. Trying to guess which households are occupied during the day can prove time-consuming and costly. Businesses able to telephone at weekends may well find that the sacrifices they make to do so are adequately rewarded. Many people leave their homes at weekends but those who are in are often more amenable than they would be if phoned during the week. No time in the evenings is automatically free of potential pitfalls. Between 6 and 7.30 pm people are recovering from a hard day's work or still driving home, children are being put to bed and meals prepared. Between 7.30 and 9pm the situation does not improve. Many are eating their supper or watching their favourite television programme. Any time after 9pm is too late. Phone calls after this time are specifically deplored by the Office of Fair Trading.

The timing of your call is especially important when phoning to obtain repeat business from existing customers. Much depends on the accuracy of the records you maintain. An analysis of the periods that have elapsed between previous orders should provide you with a clear indication of when a customer is next likely to be in the market for what you have to offer.

Annoyance

Direct mail can be collected at will and thrown away almost instantly. The telephone, however, has to be answered at a particular time. If it is ignored a business can miss valuable opportunities for new contracts and orders, and a householder long-awaited contact from valued friends and relatives. Unsolicited phone calls are thus capable of causing genuine annoyance. Some people are very busy, others feel that their privacy is being invaded or that their security is being threatened. Puzzlement as to where a number has been obtained can in particular cause considerable distress to the domestic prospect. In fact, many people feel more intimidated by a phone call out of the blue than by a visit from a door-to-door sales person because there are relatively few mysteries as to why the sales person has singled them out. He or she is walking his or her patch and calling on each household.

Always enquire whether the timing of a telephone call is convenient and recognise the right of the person to whom you are talking to end a conversation. Beware of phoning the same household more than once. Repetition of approaches that have been rejected can cause particular irritation. People who live together at the same address may well be listed separately in a phone book.

Switchboard operators

Switchboard operators and secretaries often have specific instructions not to put through unsolicited calls. The best way to get round these obstacles is to refer to literature you have sent as being the purpose behind the enquiry. Ensure that you stress the importance of the call. Your cause will be greatly enhanced if you know the exact name and title of the person to whom you wish to speak.

Market research

The phone can be used to great effect to gather information for the building of a database or to test popular opinion on a new product or service under consideration. For the latter purpose people are often surprisingly willing to cooperate. The idea that the views they are expressing may in due course lead to improvements in the product or service being discussed is doubtless partly responsible for this.

When approaching any business for market research purposes always remember that you are asking them to give up their time for no tangible reward. Every effort should thus be made to obtain the information required from the lowest level of decision-maker possible. In fact, many of the bread and butter questions could well be answered by the switchboard operator. Surveys should also be kept as brief as possible. Try to limit yourself to half a dozen questions at the most. Always remember to thank people for their cooperation.

Supporting direct mail

The phone can be used to great effect to supplement direct mail campaigns. The costs of postage are such that those indulging in expensive mailings involving brochures or catalogues can often benefit from reducing their lists to a hard core. Much can be said for composing a brief sequence along the lines demonstrated below and photocopying it in quantities sufficient to allow the necessary details to be completed during each call.

Company/Institution _____

Address _____

_____

Phone no_____

Good morning/afternoon. Could you tell me the name of the buyer/head of the _____ department/person who deals with the purchase of _____ equipment.

Name _____

Position _____

Could I also just take this opportunity to check your correct postal address (read out address, including postcode).
(After being put through)
Good morning/afternoon. My name is _____ . I am calling on behalf of _____ company about_____
_____ . If this is of sufficient interest we will shortly be sending you some information on it through the post.
(Pause for reaction.)
We will mark these details for your attention then.
(Pause to verify there is no resistance.)
Thank you for your time and I look forward to speaking to you again very soon.

Once the mailing has been sent and a suitable period has been allowed to elapse for its contents to be digested, a further phone call can be made seeking to obtain an order or to arrange an appointment for a visit from a sales representative.

Arranging appointments

The art of arranging appointments involves many of the same techniques as those used for actually selling over the telephone (as described below). It is, however, in many ways just as much an act of market research as it is of selling. The objective is to enable the time of the field force to be put to its optimum use. Appointments that are merely arranged at random will not succeed in this. Prospects must be assessed in terms of their interest and buying power as well as for their mere availability. When suitable parties have been detected, closing should take place in the form of presenting a series of alternative dates and times.

Example 1

Caller: Which day would you prefer, Tuesday or Thursday?

Prospect: Thursday.

Caller: Is morning or afternoon more convenient?

Prospect: Morning.

Caller: Shall we say 11 o'clock?

Prospect: No, I would prefer 10.30.

Caller: So our Mr Davidson will see you next Thursday, June 10th, at 10.30am.

Example 2

Caller: Our Mr Davidson is very busy for the rest of the week and he has only two times available, Thursday at 4pm or Friday at 3pm. Which of these times do you want?

Prospect: Oh, what a pity, neither of those times is suitable, but I am free for much of next week.

Caller: Which day is the most convenient?

Prospect: At the moment my diary is blank all day Wednesday.

Caller: Shall we make it 2 o'clock then?

Prospect: I would prefer 2.30, then I can guarantee that I will be back from lunch.

Caller: That's marvellous. So our Mr Davidson will see you next Wednesday, June 9th, at 2.30pm.

Telesales

Those selling over the telephone have a notable disadvantage over those who sell face to face in that their only means of communication is their voice. The bulk of contact that takes place between one human being and another is non-verbal. The telling factor in any face-to-face sale is the appearance of the sales person concerned. The telephone sales person cannot use this trump card at all. Similarly, he or she cannot interpret the body language of the prospect; for example, an involuntary leaning forward to register definite interest. Nor can well-defined graphics and illustrations be used to reinforce the key points he or she wishes to make. Despite these disadvantages, using his or her voice as the only selling tool, the telesales person is able to speak to many more prospects in any one day than his or her field sales counterpart.

Nevertheless, the twin arts require many of the same skills. Both demand a thorough knowledge of the sales person's own product and also of his or her competitors'. Enough attention must be aroused from the prospect during the first ten seconds of the presentation for the remainder to stand any chance of being effective. Once attention has been gained, securing desire, want, need and trust become urgent priorities. When these goals have been fulfilled, it still remains for the customer to be convinced both of the product's worth and of his or her ability to pay for it before an order can be taken. Finally, a sense of urgency must be created so that the prospect cannot deliver age-old lines such as 'I'd like to think about it', 'I'll call you back' or 'Why not send me some literature?'

The following points should be borne in mind by those considering a telesales campaign:

1. Traditionally, products sold entirely over the phone carry a lower price tag than most of those sold in the field. This is because prospects are understandably reluctant to part with substantial sums for something they have not actually seen and touched. There are, however, some notable exceptions to this

rule, such as advertising space, where familiarity with what is on offer tends to result in sufficient trust for transactions involving thousands of pounds to be readily conducted. In any case, the value of the sale must be commensurate with the cost of making it.

2. The longer your conversation continues, the greater the chance that the prospect's attention will wane. Try to limit your call to seven or eight minutes at the very most. Five minutes is a good average length to aim for. There is much to be said for pointing out at the start that you are intending to talk only for a brief period. Request the decision-maker's attention for 'a couple of minutes'.

3. Practice makes perfect in telesales. The more you do, the better you become. You can, however, do much to determine the rate at which you improve. At the end of each working day go over carefully every occasion on which a full presentation was made to a genuine decision-maker. Those that proved successful should receive just as much attention as those that didn't. Congratulate yourself on techniques you have employed consistently well and rigorously analyse shortcomings.

4. Keep your approach as simple as possible and be ready to adapt your style and phraseology to match the mentality of the individual to whom you are talking. Aim to speak about 20 per cent louder than you would during a normal face-to-face conversation and remember the phrase 'Smile and dial'. If you can bring a smile to your face it will be heard in your voice. Avoid talking 'at' prospects. Take the earliest opportunity to involve them in the conversation. Listen with care to what they have to say and use their comments as a guide to the direction which the next stage of your conversation should take. Sometimes prospects do not always make themselves clear when they are asking questions. It could be advantageous to repeat their questions in your own words to ensure that you are not talking at cross purposes.

5. Try to put your main benefits and unique selling points at the beginning of the conversation. If these are not attractive to a prospect your minor benefits stand even less chance of being so. You can thus save yourself valuable time by ending a conversation while it is still in its infancy. On no account persist with prospects who express no interest whatsoever. By terminating such conversations early you are not only saving

yourself the direct cost of your time and your phone bill, you are also preserving valuable mental energy. There are few more discouraging activities than continuously preaching to those who will never be converted.

6. A script (see below) can help to ensure that you do not miss any of the major points intended for discussion. It should, however, be used as a broad guide only. It must not be allowed to restrict your style or prevent you from paying due attention to the prospect. The call should flow as naturally as possible and the caller's own personality should be given a free rein. Never forget that it is invariably the sales person who is bought before the product. Sufficient familiarity with a script will ensure that it can be used conversationally and does not create an artificial tone. A script should allow for plenty of pauses but a caller should not be afraid to continue if a prospect has little to say.

7. Those with a large telesales or telemarketing requirement might be advised to consider using a telemarketing agency – see Chapter 7.

Objections

Objections are inevitable. Even if your offer is perfect and foolproof, eg if you are able to sell genuine diamond necklaces that haven't been stolen at £20 each, people will still raise objections. They are too cautious and suspicious by nature to do otherwise. The actual quantity of objections raised will, however, vary noticeably from one conversation to another. Some people will confine their resistance to points they feel are strictly pertinent. Others will go to any length to find a chink in your armour.

It is essential that any telesales operator takes a positive attitude towards the handling of objections. They should be seen not as negative statements but as expressions of interest or even as buying signals. On most occasions when they are raised, further information is being requested, or clarification is being sought of details that have already been stated. Objections are thus ideal opportunities for the caller to stress further benefits or to re-emphasise vital selling points by relating them more closely to the personal needs of the prospect.

Take all objections seriously whether they are valid or not. Whenever an objection is raised, always agree with it in the first instance. This will be particularly effective because it will be the very last reaction that the prospect is anticipating. There is much to be said for having a sheet, separate from your script, which lists answers to objections that may arise (see below).

The following are tried and tested ways of dealing with common objections.

1. Needing time to think

This objection normally means that a prospect is not entirely convinced about or happy with one or more aspects of the product or presentation.

Prospect: Well, this is certainly very interesting and I appreciate what you are saying but I never make immediate decisions, however attractive a proposition may be. Just give me one or two days to think about it and I will call you back.

Caller: Fine. I understand that you need time to think about it and many of my existing customers said exactly the same thing to me at this stage. (Agreeing with the objection.) Would I be correct in saying, Mr ———, that the fact you need time to think about it means that you must be very interested in what we've just discussed?

Prospect: Yes, that's right.

Caller: Is there anything in particular that you are not happy with? Is it _____

_____ ?

Prospect: Yes, well, actually it's the price. I think it might be too high.

Caller: So if we could clear that up then you would go ahead, would you?

Prospect: Yes, certainly.

Caller: Then do you mind me asking you, Mr ———, how much this product is worth to you as a businessman?

Prospect: I think it's worth ———.

Caller: So I take it that if it was offered at that price you would buy it?

Prospect: Yes, that's right. (He now has no alternative but to agree or lose face.)

Caller: On this occasion, I can in fact offer you the product at ——— price. How many would you like?

2. Request for literature
A request for literature is normally another way for prospects to say that they are not interested.

Prospect: Thank you very much for all this information. It certainly sounds very appealing. Send me the literature and I'll have a good look at it.

Caller: I'm glad it has proved so interesting. Many of our customers have asked for literature but I'm delighted to say that there is none and the money we have saved on this has gone towards improving the product, and this means that we can offer this quality product at a very competitive price. In fact, I can improve on impersonal literature and answer personally any further questions you may have. Is there anything in particular that you are not clear about? (Continue as in example 1.)

3. Unable to afford what's on offer
There will be cases where prospects genuinely cannot afford the product or service being offered. The majority of people, however, need to be convinced that their investment will either multiply itself many times or save them an equivalent amount.

Prospect: It sounds wonderful but unfortunately I can't afford it.

Caller: Are you saying that you cannot afford to spend X pounds on this product or do you mean that you are not convinced of its value as an investment?

Prospect: Well, you've actually just hit the nail on the head. No. I'm not in fact convinced of its value to me as an investment.

Caller: If I can show you that not only will it cover its cost but pay for itself many times over, I take it I would be correct in saying that you couldn't possibly not afford it? (The caller is establishing that the prospect must not miss this opportunity to profit substantially.)

Prospect: Yes, that sounds fair enough.

Caller: (He or she then reiterates what has gone before in the body of the presentation with regard to the worth of the product to the customer and proceeds to ask for the order once again.)

4. Not interested

This objection normally arises in the first minute of a presentation. The prospect has possibly heard a similar presentation before, has not been made fully aware of the features and benefits, and has closed his or her mind to the product or service.

Prospect: I'm afraid that I'm really not interested. (If this is said with exceptional forcefulness and aggression do not continue, but if the prospect does not sound completely convinced of his or her own lack of interest respond in the following manner.)

Caller: Can I ask you, Mr ———, exactly what it is you are not interested in?

Prospect: Well, it's not really one thing in particular. I'm just not interested. (At this point the caller must become even more enthusiastic than he was before and go straight back into his presentation, stressing the key points. If the prospect is genuinely not interested it will very soon become evident.)

5. No time available for talking

Some prospects will actually be about to leave their offices or be snowed under with work. On most occasions, however, this excuse is merely used as a brush-off line.

Prospect: Sorry, I'm afraid that I'm far too busy to talk to you.

Caller: Many of our best customers said exactly the same thing until they had a chance to hear just how superb this product really is. It will only take a couple of minutes to tell you about it. (Go straight into the presentation unless you are stopped.)

Closing

In an ideal world prospects would be so convinced of the merits of any product or service after hearing about it for the first time that it would simply be an automatic process for them to place an immediate order. Reality is, however, very different. It is human nature to find an unlimited number of reasons for not going ahead with a purchase and to show an overpowering inability to proceed with the buying process.

Some business people labour under the misconception that the recipe for success is simply to tell as many prospects as possible about their goods or services. In the world of telesales it is all too easy to fall into this trap. The most important part of any presentation over the phone is to ask for an order. A high level of proficiency in this process of closing is probably the most effective way any business can increase its sales or revenue without its staff having to leave their desks.

The following methods of closing have long been recognised as important weapons in a sales person's armoury:

1. The simplest method of closing a sale is to ask for the order in the form of a basic question which must be answered, for example:
   May we put you down for 20 cases of wine then, sir?
2. (A slight variation on 1.) The caller makes the assumption that the prospect is going to buy, for example:
   We'll put you down for 20 cases of wine then, sir?
3. The caller uses the order form as the vehicle for closing, again assuming that the prospect is going to buy, for example:
   I just need to confirm one or two details with you for the paperwork.
4. The caller gives the prospect an alternative, for example:
   Would you like to order 25 cases or only 20 this time, sir?
5. The caller runs through the advantages of going ahead with the order and asks the prospect to list them on one side of a piece of paper. He then asks the prospect to list any disadvantages. Naturally, he provides him with no help in this. The advantages

will outweigh the disadvantages and the prospective buyer is left with little choice but to place an order.

6. The caller gives the buyer a reason for going ahead today, such as an imminent price increase or a limited supply. He refers to other prospects who did not heed this advice and regretted it later. This creates a sense of urgency. It is known as 'the cautionary tale'.

7. The caller apologises and says that he must have done something wrong in his presentation because otherwise the prospect would be ready to place an order. He asks the prospect to inform him where he has made his mistake and thus uncovers his real objection. The caller isolates this objection, agrees with it and uses one of the previously mentioned closes to secure the order.

Sample script
Good morning/afternoon. Could you tell me the name of your buyer please?

Name of buyer ————

Good morning/afternoon Mr ————. My name is Trevor Hemsley. I'm calling on behalf of Nightingale Ltd, the polythene manufacturers, about a very special offer we have available on black dustbin liners.

1. I take it you do use dustbin liners?
   If reply 'yes' proceed to 2.
   If reply 'no' then continue as follows: 'I imagine that you use carrier bags, nevertheless? We have some attractive discounts available on these at the present time.'

2. We are selling dustbin liners for only £50 a thousand. That's five pence each. In fact on 5000 we can go down to four pence each. When did you last see them that cheap?

Pause for comment.

3. The offer is only on for this month because we are trying to clear our warehouse of surplus stock. We are guaranteeing to deliver within three days. In your case, in fact, we can deliver first thing tomorrow as we are loading a lorry for your area at the moment.

Pause for comment.

4. So are you interested in a single thousand or can you take five?

Quantity ———

Price ———

5. May I just check your address with you? Hooper Ltd, 4 Primrose Hill, London W11 4HP?

6. Are there any particular difficulties in finding you that the driver ought to know about?

Instructions to driver ———

7. So that's £50 plus VAT, payment on delivery.

Sample objection list

Objection 1
I can already get them for five pence each down at the market and I only have to buy five at a time.

Answer
Yes, but the bags you are getting are the flimsy kind. I expect they split on you often enough. We are offering the heavy duty type.

Objection 2
We have quite enough bags at the moment.

Answer
But it is undoubtedly worth stocking up with some more at these prices. The costs of production have been rocketing. It is now actually costing us five pence a bag to make them in the first place. It's old stock we are selling. It's not as though they take up a lot of room. For 1000 bags we are only talking about five small boxes.

Objection 3
I'll have to check with the catering department to see what our existing stock situation is like.

Answer
How long do you think it will take you to do so? Would you like me to phone you back in five minutes or would you prefer me to give you half an hour?

Objection 4
Our local council are only willing to collect the black bags they deliver which are specially printed with their name on.

Answer
Unanswerable objection. But try to interest the prospect in carrier bags.

Objection 5
We buy all our bags through the same regular supplier.

Answer
Yes, but this is a special one-off offer. We are not asking you to change suppliers, just to take advantage of an exceptionally attractive bargain which is almost certainly better value for money than can be obtained through your existing suppliers.

Mobile phones

The boom in the cellular radio industry has done much to assist the cause of those wishing to liaise with their field force without leaving their desks. The car can now become an extension of a desk. Users of mobile phones can make or receive calls in different locations of their choice within a network coverage area. The country is divided into different areas or cells, each having a base station with radio transceivers. The cells are linked to telephone exchanges which connect calls to other mobile phones and to the fixed telephone networks. When cellular subscribers make calls from their radio phones they are automatically allocated a radio channel in the local cell for their exclusive use.

There are two network operators. Vodafone, a subsidiary of Racal, and Cellnet, a joint venture between Securicor Group and British Telecom. Neither network is allowed to deal directly with the end user who must operate through a service provider or a dealer. A complete list of service providers can be obtained from both network operators. Apparatus can be bought, sold or leased. Further costs are incurred through an initial connection charge, monthly standing charge, and individual call charges. The two network operators publish details of the tariffs they charge the service providers. They in turn are free to present their own charge structures to the end user.

There are three basic categories of cellular phone. The

carphone fits into a vehicle and receives its power supply directly from the vehicle's battery. A voice activated hands-free facility can be obtained so the phone can be used without the driver having to hold the handset. The equipment can only be used in the vehicle in which it is installed. The transportable phone bears many similarities to the carphone. It is, however, designed with a detachable battery pack so it can be used outside a vehicle. Hand portables are also powered by detachable batteries. They are, however, smaller than transportables. Some models can even be fitted into a pocket.

What does it cost?

When costing a telephone sales operation you have to take into account some substantial cost factors. These are:

1. Cost of sales labour. Your sales force has to be reasonably well paid and motivated, probably earning commission on sales. There is also substantial turnover in staff, which gives you the additional expense of recruitment and training.
2. Telephone costs. These can be high, especially if you are conducting long-distance campaigns.
3. Overheads. Staff supervision, the cost of confirming sales by fax, telex or letter, premises etc.

Comparisons made with selling by direct mail have shown that the cost of making a contact by telephone can be considerably lower than by direct mail – sometimes 60 per cent lower. So what might cost £20 per contact by direct mail might cost less than £10 by telephone, but then the *conversion* of the contact might not be so easy.

As with direct mail, you must test teleselling on a small scale to see how effective it is for you with your particular product or service, before embarking on anything grander.

Points to remember

- Make sure that all staff are adequately trained to answer the phone.
- The Call Waiting Service can help to avoid the problem of engaged lines.
- Treat calls you receive with the same importance as those you make.
- Put as much of your telephone conversations as possible in writing.

- Always listen to complaints sympathetically.
- 0800 and Freefone numbers can greatly improve response.
- Don't be afraid to put your phone calls to more than one purpose.
- Take every opportunity to avoid spending unnecessary time on the phone.
- Never attempt to make sales calls under the guise of market research.
- Test different approaches.
- Phoning is a numbers game; organisation is therefore essential.
- Choosing the correct time to phone can be vitally important.
- Unsolicited phone calls can cause genuine annoyance.
- Arranging appointments is an act of market research as well as selling.
- Five minutes is a good average length of sales call for which to aim.
- A script should be used as a broad guide only.
- Take a positive attitude towards objections.
- Never underestimate the importance of effective closing.
- Cellular radio has enabled a car to become an extension of a desk.
- Check your telephone costs regularly.

5
Advertising

If you have difficulty in understanding why so much money is spent on advertising you can rest assured you are not alone. A great many people share your puzzlement. The reason is, however, straightforward. It is simply because advertising works.

The questions of how, why and when it works are far less easy to answer. Even those with the greatest expertise are unable to predict exactly which part of their advertising expenditure is likely to have the greatest impact on increasing their sales. Response to individual advertisements is highly unpredictable. Identical advertisements broadcast or published at exactly the same time on consecutive days can produce markedly different results.

Those organisations which can afford to spend millions of pounds on advertising can counteract these problems to a certain extent by sheer quantity of activity. Many of the peaks and troughs involved will even out during the course of several large-scale campaigns. For smaller business people, however, the margin for error is invariably much tighter. They must concentrate on designing advertisements that can stimulate an immediate response, and on placing them where they are most likely to reach the desired target audience.

The considerable growth of advertising opportunities within local media has helped greatly. Activities need not be confined to the press alone. Radio and TV are within reach of those with a few thousand pounds to spend. Advertisers do not have to leave their desks in order to make the commercials that are required. Most stations are able to perform the task on their client's behalf either through their own creative departments or third parties.

There are no set rules regarding whether or not a business should advertise. Indeed, in some cases, where a company has a ready market for its goods or services, it may be quite unnecessary to consider doing so at all. Many of the decisions involved with the designing and placing of advertisements are also largely subjective. The following guidelines should, however, do much to help the uninitiated.

Law

The general principles of the British Code of Advertising Practice (Section B) are reproduced in the Appendix. Anyone intending to do their own advertising should obtain a copy of the Code itself. It contains detailed rules applicable to particular categories of advertisement such as mail order, slimming and cosmetics. If you offer incentives you will need also to obtain a copy of the British Code of Sales Promotion Practice. Both can be obtained free of charge from:

> The Advertising Standards Authority
> Brook House
> 2–16 Torrington Place
> London WC1E 7HN
> Tel: 071-580 5555

Both Codes cover printed and cinema advertising but are not responsible for radio or TV commercials. Close links are nevertheless kept with these media so that various sets of controls are kept in line with one another.

If you do not abide by the law you will undoubtedly find that the situation will catch up with you. Those with whom you advertise are likely to report untruthful or dubious claims. Even those ads that slip through the net are likely to have their own commercial repercussions. People are constantly on their guard against unrealistic claims. If you have any doubts whether or not you have interpreted the law correctly you should send a copy of your advertisement to The Advertising Standards Authority. They will happily vet it for you free of charge.

There is much to be said for including a suitable money-back guarantee in all your advertising. This can do much to inspire confidence in what you are offering. It can also act as a useful guide to whether your product is viable.

Control of message

Advertising, unlike PR, enables a business to tailor the contents of its message to suit its own requirements and to determine when and where that message appears. This is a vitally important attribute and should be exploited to the full. If money is to be spent on space or air time the contents, timing and positioning of the advertisement should receive due consideration. Paying for the space is only half the battle. What use you make of the space you have bought is up to you. It may cost you extra to achieve exactly the effect you are seeking, but the additional outlay is invariably worth while. The space you have purchased will not come any cheaper just because you fail to put it to optimum use.

Demanding attention

You have no right to demand that people read, listen to or watch your advertisements. The task of capturing and holding their attention is yours. You have paid for the privilege of delivering a sales message, so make sure that you do so. Your potential customers must be left in no doubt what it is you are intending to sell them and how they will benefit from it. Be direct in what you are saying and don't be afraid to make promises which you can substantiate. Be wary, however, of merely presenting tedious lists of selling points. Try to use everyday language wherever possible. Much of the effort you have devoted to locating the right target audience will have been wasted unless virtually all of them can understand what you are saying.

Repetition

Advertising rarely works well on a one-off basis. Repetition is essential if its optimum benefits are to be realised and a series of small advertisements is likely to be more effective than one large one. Try not to confine your message to one medium. You might find that your local newspaper, TV and radio stations provide access to many of the same people. Emphasise the same major themes and unique selling points from a variety of different angles. If you can think of a catchy jingle or phrase then stick with it. Use it in all your advertisements. The more often it is heard the more effective it is likely to become.

Make it easy to respond

Try to make it as easy as possible for the recipients to respond. Include an address or telephone number to which they can reply. Consider using the Freepost and Freefone facilities described in Chapters 3 and 4 to this end. Make the prices and methods of payment involved entirely clear. Say whether or not VAT is included. Is there an extra charge for postage and packing? State to whom cheques or postal orders should be made payable. Highlight the facility to pay by credit card.

Test the market

The best deals in advertising invariably arise through the booking of a large series of advertisements. Ensure, however, that you never lay out substantial sums of money until you have tested the market with a small series. The process has not ended once you are satisfied that your existing campaigns are proving profitable. Always be on the lookout for uncovering potentially more lucrative areas of demand. Carry out tests in response to ideas that you feel are appropriate. Keep an eye out in particular for new advertising campaigns being conducted by your competitors.

Organisation

Ensure that you keep detailed schedules of all forthcoming advertisements so that the necessary back-up facilities can be arranged. Record full details of all who respond to your advertisements. Not just those who buy from you. Anyone who has made the effort to express initial interest should be regarded as a valuable future lead. Keep detailed records of all correspondence with advertising sales departments. Get into the habit of confirming all bookings that you make in writing. Ensure those you deal with do likewise – especially when they offer favourable terms. There is nothing worse than trying to sort out misunderstandings at the invoice stage.

Look out for opportunities

Always be on the lookout for bargains. The following opportunities should not be missed:

1. Any booking of a series of advertisements should involve attractive discounts. Don't be afraid to drive a hard bargain. Make a point of not taking initial quotes at face value.
2. There are sometimes opportunities to obtain free editorial with advertising.
3. If you are mentioned in press editorial matter there is much to be said for taking out an advertisement in the same issue. Its value for money is likely to prove above average. Many publications actually make a point of contacting companies mentioned

in editorial directly to see if they wish to advertise.

4. Look out for publications in difficulty. Most magazines are dependent on advertising revenue to the extent that their very existence can be threatened by trends which lead companies to cut back on advertising. In such times space may be available at ridiculously cheap rates while readership levels remain broadly constant.

Interpreting response

All advertisements that include some form of response device will provide you with direct indications of their cost-effectiveness. Make sure, however, that you are in a position to determine which replies come from which advertisements. The most effective way of doing this is to allocate a separate reference to each advertisement and request that this should be quoted in replies, or have it printed on the reply coupon. Give each publication or other advertising outlet its own letter of the alphabet and each advertisement that you place with it a specific number (ie, F6 will refer to the sixth advertisement that you have placed in publication F).

If you have a clear idea of the basic profit margin for your product you will know roughly how many sales are necessary for an advertisement to pay its way. If, for example, your product is being sold at £25 and you know that it cost you £15 to produce, then the basic profit margin is £10. An advertisement costing £500 will in theory need 50 sales to break even. The following points should, however, be borne in mind when seeking to establish an advertisement's cost-effectiveness.

1. The cost of the back-up service necessary to secure the sale, ie labour, administration, leaflets and brochures and postage, will reduce this £10 margin.

2. On the other hand, repeat business, recommendation, useful future leads from unconverted enquiries, and the part your advertisement plays within the context of your overall campaign will all enhance this margin.

Advertising rates

All the initial information that you need to obtain on advertising rates for the vast majority of available publications and other types of media can be obtained from one source. This is called

BRAD (*British Rate and Data*). It provides details of advertising rates, page sizes, contact names, addresses, telephone numbers, circulation figures and a host of other useful information. Because it is revised monthly the information that it contains stands every chance of being accurate and up to date. Before every new edition all publications mentioned receive a reproduction of their entries to correct or amend. If this is not returned the entry is repeated from the previous edition. Those publications not responding within one year are contacted personally.

The cost of 12 monthly editions of *BRAD* is £300. This covers postage and packing. The cost of a single edition in isolation is £115. *BRAD* is published by:

Maclean Hunter Limited
Maclean Hunter House
Chalk Lane
Cockfosters Road
Barnet
Herts EN4 0BU
Tel: 081-975 9759

Press advertising

The chief attractions of press advertising are as follows:

1. Choice
A huge number of publications, many of them with highly specialist readerships. This provides clear opportunities for those who seek accurate targeting.

2. Timing
Particularly good opportunities for exercising skill in timing. Advertisements can be booked well in advance to coincide with other developments in sales and marketing strategy. Those products with strong seasonal or topical appeal can enjoy valuable affinity with editorial matter that greatly adds to their interest.

3. Cost
Sizeable advertisements can be placed in many respectable publications for only a few hundred pounds. This means that those with relatively limited resources can afford to make their presence felt by concentrating on a particular industry or limited

geographical area. Ideas for large and less easily quantifiable campaigns can also be tested inexpensively.

4. Permanence of message

Daily papers are invariably discarded within 24 hours and replies to advertisements that they contain are normally made on the day of publication. In the case of weekly or monthly publications, however, response tends to be spread over a longer period. This can be particularly useful for the very small business as it enables existing staffing levels to cope with the additional enquiries.

Those publications that are issued monthly or less frequently can in fact provoke response several years after the date of the advertisement. They are often kept for reference purposes. Advertisements placed in yearbooks and other annual publications and directories can also have this effect. The actual advertising value of some of these is, however, very much open to question. Those who are intent on advertising in a directory would probably minimise their risks by sticking with Yellow Pages or their Thomson Local Directory. At least they can be assured that readers are actively in the market for what they have to offer, although specialist directories will be much more accurately targeted.

5. Greater detail

The opportunities to explain points in detail are considerably greater in the press than can be achieved through sound and vision. The press is thus a highly suitable medium for promoting those products and concepts which are highly technical or difficult to understand. Even if the message isn't immediately comprehended the reader has the chance to re-read.

This ability to create greater detail is particularly important when it comes to incorporating suitable response devices. There is no time limit in which full postal addresses and telephone numbers have to be digested. Brief questionnaires can be included in coupon reply services and the information from these used to build up a database for exploitation in future campaigns.

6. Greater control

Because you have extensive knowledge of your product you are often in a good position to write your own copy. If you have selected a suitable designer you should be able to compose all your press advertising without having to leave your desk. In the case of radio, cinema and TV, however, you will normally be dependent on other people to create the required formats on your behalf. The level of thought and skill that they exercise could leave something to be desired. Many publications will offer to prepare your artwork inexpensively. Nevertheless, if you are confident in what you can produce there is much to be said for doing it yourself.

Those indulging in press advertising should pay particular attention to the following points:

Circulation

A publication's circulation figures can cast much useful light on the value for money that you are likely to achieve from your advertisement. It should be remembered, however, (as discussed in Chapter 6) that a copy of one publication might be read by several people whereas a substantial number of copies of another might not be read at all. It is not always wise to take publications' own estimates of their circulations at face value. More often than not their figures will have been checked by an external organisation. The vast majority of newspaper and magazine circulations in the UK are verified by ABC, an independent bureau which operates a random inspection of publishers' records. The circulations of many free publications are verified by its subsidiary VFD. Latest ABC and VFD figures are automatically passed to *BRAD*.

Rates and bookings

The advertising rates published in *BRAD* will provide you with a useful guide to what you can expect to pay for advertisements in any particular publications. For any advertiser who pays due attention to budgeting, however, this information should act as no more than a starting point. Your next step should be to contact the advertising departments of those publications in which you have a serious interest. Ask them to send you a specimen copy along with a rate card.

Study the specimen copy to see what other types of organisation use it to advertise. Does it include the names of well established companies? If so, are they just using it for image building or are they incorporating response devices to sell directly? Are any of your major competitors advertising in it? If they are, study their advertisements to see exactly what they are aiming to achieve. If your proposed copy is too similar to theirs, give further thought to how you can improve it. Insert some vital distinguishing features.

Examine the positions in which advertisements appear. Are they mostly grouped together in the back? If so that's exactly where you don't want to be! You've got far more chance of having your advertisement seen if you are placed next to a piece of editorial. You need to determine whether the advertising department can guarantee you a place in such a position on a regular basis and whether there is any extra charge involved for the privilege. Look out for any regular columns or slots that could prove pertinent to your advertising needs. If, for example, you are aiming at a male audience you may benefit from appearing in a sport or business section. If you are trying to reach women a fashion page is likely to be more suitable. The actual place on a page where an advertisement appears can also be important. You need to make sure that your message appears in a position where it is most likely to be seen. The top right-hand corner of a right-hand page is considered by many to represent an ideal slot.

Once you have established a comprehensive list of further questions that you wish to ask you should recontact the relevant advertising department. You may well find that one of their sales reps has already booked an appointment to come to see you. Be sure to establish whether rates include VAT. Check that they will allow you to cancel your advertisements free of charge if suitable notice is given. This power to cancel will ensure that you are able to make preliminary bookings while testing the market. If the publication's circulation figures have not been independently verified ask them why.

It is only after you have explored some potential sources of advertising in depth that you are in a position to make any serious comparisons.

Content

Opportunities to sell 'off-the-page' through the press can be divided into two main categories – those advertisements which seek to sell directly and those which are aiming to encourage a request for further information. For the small-time advertiser the former method is likely to prove most cost-effective. With two-stage selling there is usually a substantial drop-off effect between the number of initial enquiries and the number of sales that actually result. It is thus most suitable for those organisations selling products involving the outlay of large amounts of money and/or seeking to build a database for the purposes of long-term development.

An advertisement for a one-stage sale must provide the potential purchaser with all the information necessary for a buying decision to be reached, taking great care to avoid unnecessary wording. It has been estimated that the average reader spends as little as one second looking at any one advertisement. Capturing his initial attention is thus quite a challenge. Despite this, the level of imagination shown by most advertisers in the presentation and content of their material is extremely low. A good heading can work wonders in arousing interest. Keep it short. Make it rhyme if possible. Illustrations can also prove effective for this purpose.

Display advertisements in the national press which invite readers to send money must be approved by the Mail Order Protection Scheme (MOPS). Advertisers are vetted so that their status and integrity in business may be confirmed. Information is available from:

Mail Order Protection Scheme
Newspaper Publishers Association Ltd
16 Took's Court
London EC4A 1LB
Tel: 071-405 6806

Response devices

Try to provide the reader with the option to reply either by post or telephone. The telephone has obvious attractions in terms of convenience as a means of response, particularly if Freefone or 0800 facilities are available (see Chapter 4). A great many consumers will always prefer to reply by post. The idea that undue pressure may be exerted on them during the course of a telephone conversation often has much to do with this. Business customers are ordering on an increasing scale by fax.

Try to include a coupon that can be cut out and returned for the reply. Make sure that it is as clear, precise and easy to fill in as possible. Stick to the same basic format each time you advertise, so people become used to your approach. Try to include questions that can provide you with valuable information for your database, such as the recipient's age and preferred title. Always ensure that the coupon is taken into consideration from the outset when designing an advertisement so that it is effectively integrated with the remainder of the material. The coupon must be placed in a position where it is immediately evident and at the same time be easy to cut out. The middle of an advertisement is therefore clearly unsuitable, and it must not be backed by another advertiser's coupon or, in serious journals, by text that the reader will want to keep for reference.

Inserts

Inserts – either loose or attached – can provide a valuable alternative or supplement to conventional 'off-the-page' advertising. They can be used to great effect to test ideas inexpensively by sending them to only a selection of a publication's audience. They can also offer the opportunity to advertise in media that do not actually carry page space advertising and to negotiate more attractive rates from those titles where advertising space is prohibitively expensive.

A good general purpose insert can serve a wide range of different functions. It can be placed in your catalogue, included in deliveries of goods for which sales have already been made and despatched in direct mailing exercises.

An insert's main strength lies in the fact that its presence is normally abundantly obvious. Readers do not normally have to stumble across it. More often than not a loose insert will fall straight on to their laps when they open a magazine. A suitable impression will, however, only be made if due skill is exercised. Much depends on making effective use of eye-catching illustrations and photographs.

Cinema

The fact that most cinemas contain between 100 and 1000 seats places notable restrictions on the size of audience they permit an advertiser to reach. Nevertheless, people are often at their most receptive while at the cinema. They have, after all, had to make a conscious effort to attend. The following other advantages should also be considered:

1. Advertising rates are very competitive. A weekly outlay of £15 to £40 can secure about 20 brief slots a week (booked over a period of a year or more).
2. Local inhabitants constitute a significant proportion of most cinema audiences. This can be particularly useful for stressing the presence of a local shop or premises.

About three-quarters of cinema advertising rights in the UK are owned by Rank Screen Advertising (tel 071-439 9531) and the vast majority of the remainder by Pearl and Dean (tel 071-262 5000). Those seeking to advertise sho ld get in touch with the relevant sales departments. You should notice which group your cinema falls under by paying attention to existing commercials. Alternatively, you may find that pre-paid advertising cards are available in the foyer. If in doubt ask at the box office.

If you wish to show only the most basic kind of advertisement there is no need to consider having to leave your desk. Rank Screen Advertising has a library of several thousand ready-made stock commercials to which they can simply add a new advertiser's name and address. No charge is made for the service if a series of advertisements is booked.

Pearl and Dean also has a stock library, but relatively little use is now made of this. By means of a computer graphics machine it is able to make a simple commercial from photographs supplied by the client and an accompanying voice-over. The cost for the service is often as little as £250. Its own photographer is available to visit you for an additional charge.

Radio

Advertising on independent local radio can prove advantageous for the following reasons:

1. It can reach people where many other forms of advertising cannot. People listen to their radios in their cars, gardens, baths and in virtually every household situation.
2. The fact that most listeners have become familiar with their regular broadcasters and disc jockeys means that they tend to greet what they hear with an above average degree of trust.
3. Rates are far from prohibitively expensive. Some provincial stations can create a commercial and broadcast it in some 20 half-minute slots for as little as £1000. Even in London £2000 can be sufficient to conduct a reasonable trial campaign.
4. Music, voice-overs and other sound effects can be exploited to match the tastes of a particular intended target audience.

Targeting

Air time is subdivided into time slots. Their prices reflect the number of people that is likely to be reached at that particular time. Peak-time, for example, generally occurs between 7 and 9am when audiences are boosted by people listening while eating breakfast or travelling to work by car. Some off-peak slots can represent particularly strong attractions to those seeking to approach housewives or other specialist audiences. Many of the keenest rates are available by purchasing a package of advertisements which provides coverage at different points in the day on a basis of so many slots per week. Much of the effectiveness of these, however, depends on the extent to which the advertising staff are prepared to honour requests for advertisements to be broadcast at particular times.

The bulk of opportunities on radio is for those who wish to promote products with general public appeal by capturing people during their leisure time. Business to business advertising can, however, be performed effectively by aiming at drivers on their way to work. Remember, though, that drivers on the move are unable to note down names and addresses and that their attention is easily diverted by their task in hand. The emphasis must be on using response devices that are easily remembered. Freefone numbers (see Chapter 4) are particularly suitable for this purpose.

Format
The need for repetition is even greater than in the case of press advertising. People tend to take a casual approach to their radio listening. More often that not they are using the radio as background entertainment while relaxing or concentrating on household chores. Ten-second slots are ideal for the constant repetition of brief messages. Longer commercials are often necessary to provide detailed supplementary descriptions.

Television
The principal advantages of advertising on independent television are as follows:

1. Freedom of expression
The advertiser can make use of sound, colour, movement and virtually any technique that is capable of capturing and maintaining a viewer's attention.

2. Size of audience
Far more people can be reached at any one time than through any

other medium. Catchment areas are vast. Your local TV station is likely to be watched by several million people during the course of any one week. An audience at a peak viewing time will probably fill Wembley Stadium many times over.

3. Prestige

Advertising on television can provide a business with valuable prestige. Although some advertising rates are relatively inexpensive the majority of viewers are not aware of this.

4. Sophisticated facilities

The support facilities that an independent television station is able to offer its advertisers are likely to be greater than elsewhere. Market research into viewing habits, in particular, can provide valuable clues for targeting purposes. This is capable of being highly detailed. Those living in the Thames area, for example, can obtain information as specific as the fact that 77 per cent of the Thames adult population have a bank account and 38 per cent of households in the Thames area have a fridge freezer.

5. Commands attention

Radio and press advertisements are all too easily ignored. The fact that a TV screen projects directly into a viewer's living room and that many audiences are specifically making a conscious effort to watch a particular programme greatly reduces such problems.

6. Suitability

Independent television stations have been making considerable efforts to provide advertising opportunities for the smaller business. Local rate cards offering favourable terms are now commonplace. Some of them purport to provide cheaper advertising than can be obtained in the press. Indeed, with some provincial stations £1000 can secure the production of a still commercial and a voice-over, together with its showing in seven or eight peak 10-second slots. Once cable TV has gained full momentum opportunities may well become less expensive still.

Those seeking to make full use of the advantages presented by television as an advertising medium should, however, be thinking in terms of spending tens of thousands of pounds. In such circumstances the advantage of operating through an advertising agent or media independent should be seriously considered (see Chapter 7).

Sales promotion

Competitions

A growing number of firms are now launching their own competitions in order to draw attention to products and services in general terms and to highlight specific issues. A competition can be used with particular effect in the following areas:

1. Its presence in a catalogue can significantly enhance readership.
2. If suitably advertised on a label it can greatly increase the appeal of individual products at particular times.
3. If run in conjunction with a local newspaper it can do much to draw attention to a firm's presence within the community.
4. It can provide useful supplements for direct mailing campaigns (see Chapter 3).
5. Imparting news of a competition can provide an excellent reason for getting in touch with existing customers.

Advantages and disadvantages

Replies to competitions can provide valuable information for the purposes of building a database. Those requiring entrants to produce slogans can generate useful ideas for future promotional material. Nevertheless, competitions require a great deal of time and effort on the part of the consumer and are no more than a vehicle for publicity. A great many entrants will be more interested in your competition than in your product. Some may well be people who make a living from doing nothing but entering competitions.

Law

The rules and regulations governing the use of competitions are extremely rigorous. Anyone considering entering this field should therefore obtain a copy of The British Code of Sales Promotion Practice in which rules for competitions are explicitly laid down. When you have completed designing your competition always submit a copy of it to the Advertising Standards Authority before you indulge in any designing or printing.

Format

Try to make your competition unusual and interesting rather than difficult. Your aim is, after all, to get as many people as possible to enter. The more chance they think they have of winning and the less effort that they have to put in, then the greater are the chances that they will be interested. A proven format is to ask a series of questions which are relatively easy to answer and to demand that entries are accompanied by a slogan on a specified subject which will act as a 'Tie Breaker'.

There is much to be said for making your main prize relevant to your product range or field of business. This way you will ensure that the bulk of your entries provides you with leads from people with a specific taste. Try to include a large number of smaller runner-up prizes. These should greatly increase the chances that people feel they have of winning something.

Other forms of sales promotion

The launching of a competition is just one example of a range of options to stimulate interest in your company or goods by means of offering direct incentives. Discounts, vouchers, and free gifts are among the other most commonly exploited methods. All fall under the heading of sales promotion and are subject to specific rules in the British Code of Sales Promotion Practice.

If you are seeking to enter the field of sales promotion in a big way it might well be worth your while considering a specialist sales promotion consultancy to act on your behalf (see Chapter 7). A useful book on the subject is *Sales Promotion* by Julian Cummins (Kogan Page).

Points to remember

- Obtain a copy of (a) British Code of Advertising Practice; (b) British Code of Sales Promotion Practice.
- The Advertising Standards Authority will happily vet advertisements.
- A suitable money-back guarantee can do much to win consumer confidence.
- Most advertising depends on repetition to be truly effective.
- Make it as easy as possible for people to respond to your advertisements.
- Always test the market before embarking on large-scale campaigns.
- Make sure you monitor response by coding reply addresses and coupons.
- Be on the lookout for bargains.
- Obtain a copy of *BRAD*.

- Ask for specimen copies of publications in which you are interested.
- A good heading can work wonders in arousing interest.

6
Getting Free Publicity

Public relations (PR) is, in its broadest sense, the art of building goodwill. More often than not the term PR is used specifically to describe those efforts made by a business to increase its exposure to the general public by obtaining media coverage. The publicity can often be obtained free of charge, unlike the advertising methods described in Chapter 5. It is, nevertheless, often the result of considerable effort and other indirect forms of expense.

Staying close to your desk places certain restrictions on the types of public relations campaigns that you are able to conduct personally. You cannot, for example, indulge in or attend many conventional forms of business entertainment, supervise exhibitions or conduct conferences and seminars – although you can contract a PR consultancy to take care of some of these activities on your behalf (see Chapter 7). Mercifully, however, the art of obtaining media coverage is tailor-made to be carried out from your desk.

Obtaining media coverage

Contrary to popular belief, the most effective way for the majority of businesses to increase their exposure to the media is not to provide journalists with constant invitations to meetings, lunches or other social occasions. They are often far too busy to attend unless the event focuses on a matter of exceptional importance or topical interest. Deadlines and profit margins are tight.

Far greater success is likely to be obtained through the submission of suitable information in a format that can be readily used. High standards of accuracy, presentation and punctuality are more favourably remembered than hours wasted at functions that provided three-line news items.

Benefits of obtaining media coverage

Media coverage can increase a company's sales both directly and indirectly. It can be employed with great effect to increase public awareness of an organisation's or product's existence. When the consumer comes across the company or product at a later date, either by chance or as a result of direct advertising, this prior publicity can play a valuable part in ensuring that his curiosity is aroused. Most forms of advertising depend on repetition to be truly effective (see Chapter 5). The same principle applies to editorial coverage. The more frequently a name is mentioned, the greater the significance it tends to assume in the mind of the potential purchaser. The process is often subconscious. The media can also be successfully used to realise more specific goals such as cultivating a company's image within its home town or highlighting particular individual features, issues and manoeuvres.

Advantages

Editorial coverage has the following notable advantages over advertising:

1. No charge is made for the publicity.
2. In the case of written material there is far greater chance that the reference will actually be seen. Many people will read an article in its entirety. Few will do anything other than skim advertisements.
3. The sentiment that is conveyed is more likely to be accepted as true. The journalists are expressing independent views and the public tends to react more favourably to publicity that hasn't been paid for.
4. The results of media mentions can often be quite staggering, especially if you are fortunate enough to make it in the national press.

Disadvantages

The following disadvantages must nevertheless be considered:

1. You have no automatic right to editorial coverage and have only very limited control over what appears, when it appears or where it is positioned.
2. There is no facility to incorporate direct response mechanisms.
3. The effectiveness of your efforts is extremely difficult to quantify. Even if you are able to keep accurate records of the mentions that you receive you are still faced with the fact that

their significance cannot be measured solely in terms of the volumes of words that have been used. The exact part that individual items (or even entire public relations campaigns) play in increasing your sales will always remain something of a mystery.

4. There is the possibility that you will receive indifferent or unfavourable publicity. In practice, however, swipes at companies do not occur all that frequently. When they do, they are often the result of personal grievances. It is also worth bearing in mind that there is much truth in the saying that 'any publicity is good publicity'. A company's presence in the news can add to its stature even if controversial side effects are involved.

Getting written up in the press

The vast majority of opportunities for the smaller business person to exploit the benefits of free media coverage lie in the press. With well over 10,000 different magazines, newspapers and other journals being published in the UK the chances of appearing in print are now greater than ever. Many titles have a distinctly regional or specialist stance and thus enable specific audiences to be addressed.

Publications differ noticeably in format, style, objective and an abundance of other different ways. Some are paid for while others are issued free of charge. Some are available in shops, others only by private subscription. Some are produced daily, others weekly, monthly, quarterly or even less frequently. Most, however, fall within one of the following broad groups:

1. National press
2. Consumer magazines
3. Trade and technical press
4. Local press

It is within the last two categories in particular that many smaller businesses fail to explore important avenues for obtaining valuable publicity.

Local press

Local newspapers, unlike the national press, specifically seek editorial content of strong local interest. The chances of getting such material accepted in the first place are therefore much greater. A mention in a good local newspaper with a circulation of around 100,000 could reach the attention of far more potential customers that the same mention in a national paper with a readership of well over a million.

Trade press

Far more people read trade publications than is generally realised. An individual copy is often circulated to an entire department and read from cover to cover by three or four of its members. A mention in a trade magazine with a circulation of only a couple of thousand could result in far more sales than one in a highly fashionable glossy magazine. The latter may well sit on prestigious coffee tables without ever being read. The trade magazine is likely to enjoy a higher readership per copy and offer the considerable advantage that every reader has a direct interest in the field of business in which the contributor is operating.

The budgets, and therefore the staff numbers, of trade magazines are often very limited, which means that they tend to make a higher than average use of outside contributions. The contents of some are even produced by an editor in isolation. This is not always obvious because honorary titles may be allocated to regular freelance contributors or to members of staff within the same publishing group, whose involvement is only minimal. Furthermore, the number of people who have the specialist knowledge necessary to provide the standard of information they are seeking is often very limited.

Choosing suitable material

There are few magazines or newspapers that don't consider outside contributions. Even those with large in-house teams of staff and access to sophisticated external news services still use their fair share of unsolicited information. Indeed, to a certain extent they actually depend on it. They are, nevertheless, rarely short of material from which to choose.

Your initial challenge is twofold. First, if you are to stand any chance at all of getting items accepted you must submit matter which is likely to be of interest to a significant proportion of the readers. Second, your submissions must be of greater interest than the vast majority of other items from which the editorial team can choose.

Presenting unsuitable material is merely a waste of your

resources. It can also greatly reduce the chances of future, more suitable pieces, receiving adequate consideration from the same editors. Success largely depends on the skill exercised in choosing appropriate material and suitable publications. There is nothing more negative in the field of PR than targeting a journalist for its own sake.

Most material that is used can be described as either news items or features. On the whole, daily or weekly publications have a strong news bias, while those issued monthly or even less frequently tend to be feature orientated.

News items

News rooms are rarely short of news. They are inundated. Indeed, news editors of major publications are sometimes evaluating as many as 50 or 60 different news stories a minute. Nevertheless, among the local and trade press competition is often less intense, and items of genuine interest stand a realistic chance of getting accepted.

The most effective way of submitting news material is by means of a press release. Many of the considerations involved in preparing this effectively are outlined below. Bear in mind that there is a certain amount of luck as well as skill involved. Publications may well have an embarrassment of riches available for some issues whereas at other times their choices are limited.

Avoid the temptation to push non-news items and ensure that your story is angled to match the requirements of different markets. Suitable news items can often result from the following areas:

1. A move into a new field of business
2. The launch of a new product
3. A change of headquarters or opening/closure of other premises or operations – especially if large numbers of jobs are created or lost
4. Acquisitions
5. Significant promotions and appointments
6. Sponsorships or other charitable undertakings
7. The winning of major new contracts.

Features

Some feature articles are written in-house while others are

provided by outside contributors. The latter are often specifically commissioned from professional freelance writers or experts in particular fields. The use made of material that arrives out of the blue tends to be limited in comparison. Even if its style and content offer strong appeal there is always the possibility that it may not be factually correct.

A businessman who feels that he has a particularly good idea for an article might find it worth making an exploratory telephone call to the features editor of a relevant publication. If the enquiry stimulates sufficient interest a brief written synopsis of the intended feature may well be requested. Should the features editor wish to proceed any further he will issue guidelines concerning length, deadline and subject matter. If you have particular specialist knowledge you may even find that a trade publication is prepared to offer you a regular column.

Never be tempted to write an article which is clearly advertorial in nature. It is most unlikely to be accepted as editorial matter. Even those that slip through the net will probably not yield the same benefits as well balanced articles incorporating subtle references to your company. Too much flattery tends to make readers switch off. Try to mention your company no more than twice directly. If people enjoy reading the article this should be sufficient to provide the publicity you are seeking.

It is also a good idea to try to get involved with articles that are to be written by other people. Most magazines issue lists of forthcoming features that can be obtained upon request. If you feel that you might be able to contribute to these by providing interesting opinions or other useful information, make a point of getting in touch. Issue a press release that is of direct relevance to the subject in hand. This might entice the writer to quote you directly or to contact you for a more detailed discussion.

The following opportunities for obtaining coverage in feature articles should be looked out for:

1. Emphasising new, unusual or market-leading products in surveys and industry overviews
2. Promoting products with strong seasonal or topical appeal
3. Explaining the stance a company is taking on a matter of contemporary importance.

Researching the market

Publications that you subscribe to regularly should be studied carefully. Familiarise yourself with their subject matter and see what has already been covered in the recent past. These will, however, represent only a tiny proportion of your exposure potential. You must aim to spread your message across as broad a spectrum as possible. There is no need to leave your desk to visit a reference library to obtain details of magazines and newspapers. There are a number of sources which list the possible options. The most established of these are *PR Planner* (updated monthly, £195 per annum), *PIMS UK Media Directory* (published monthly, £240 per annum), *PNA Media Guide* (published bi-monthly, £170 per annum for six issues) and *Editors Media Directories* (updated monthly, £295 per annum for all six volumes).

Initial steps

1. Draw up a list of all the publications which you feel might be interested in what you have to offer.
2. Make a phone call to each to check on the following points:
   (a) That addresses and names of relevant editors, news editors or features editors are still up to date.
       The publishing world is in a constant state of flux. Newspapers and magazines are forever folding and editorial titles changing. One of the most common complaints that journalists express about the PR material they receive is that it is addressed to an editor who left several months previously.
   (b) The deadline date for receipt of copy to be considered for a particular issue.
       As a broad rule deadlines tend to be as follows:

       Dailies – not later than 4.30pm the day before, even for the hottest news items
       Weeklies – seven days before
       Monthlies – between six weeks and three months before.
   (c) The type of photographs that can be used.
       A growing number of trade magazines are now using colour photographs.
3. Prepare press releases tailored to suit each publication. In some cases you will be able to use an almost identical format to approach a handful of editors. Ensure, however, that you are always on the lookout for ways of adjusting what you have to say to suit individual requirements.

The press release

A well-designed press release can save a journalist a considerable amount of time. While you are trying to increase your sales without leaving your desk the journalist will be trying to maximise his productivity without leaving *his* desk. Providing him with suitable news and feature material can greatly reduce the amount of time that he has to spend on interviews and other forms of research.

Your submission must stand out from the crowd. Competition is fierce. The average newspaper editor wades through a pile of press releases over a foot high every working day. Most of them end up in the waste paper basket. They are often poorly researched and clumsily written.

Adherence to the following guidelines will greatly increase the chances of your releases being accepted:

1. Make sure that the contents are kept as short and straightforward as possible.
2. Type on one side of the page only and always use double spacing.
3. Ensure that you include a name and telephone number that can be contacted for further information.
4. Always incorporate a brief eye-catching headline.
5. Present information in descending order of importance so that all the major details are in the first couple of paragraphs.
6. Always include those dates when you would prefer the information to be released. Don't forget also the actual date of writing.
7. Make sure that any quotes used are from the most senior personnel available.
8. Do not include any information if you have the slightest doubt of its accuracy.

Do not be tempted to enclose leaflets or brochures with the press release. If the journalists require further information they will get in touch with you. On some occasions they might wish merely to ask brief questions for purposes of clarification. On others they might want to develop aspects of your story in more detail. Never telephone yourself to enquire whether a particular release is going to be used. (Some examples of press releases prepared by a leading PR consultancy are shown in Chapter 7.)

Photographs

The inclusion of an attractive photograph can greatly increase both the chances that your material will be used and the likelihood that it will subsequently be read. The following guidelines should be noted:

1. Make sure the photograph is clear and easily reproducible.
2. Enclose a caption referring to the contents of the photograph. Ensure that this includes the names of any people shown. Captions can be stuck on the back.
3. Be wary of marring the quality of the photograph. Avoid using staples or other fasteners. Always deliver in a stiff, hard-backed envelope with 'Please Do Not Bend' written on the outside.
4. Keep duplicates of any photographs that you submit.
5. Aim to be imaginative in the way that products are presented. Avoid straightforward snapshots. Try to include in the shot people or other items likely to command attention.
6. If possible, always submit a variety of photographs from which an editor can select the ones he feels are most suitable.

Building relationships with the press

The development of good long-term relationships with particular publications or journalists can do much to arouse their attention to the merits of a particular story. A rapport with a good freelance can be especially worthwhile. They are generally in contact with a number of different publications and are thus able to exploit opportunities on your behalf. Many of the secrets of building such relationships lie in maintaining consistently high standards of accuracy and reliability. Pay particular attention to the following:

1. Avoid making assumptions about your own importance even if you are a regular contributor or advertiser with a publication.
2. Always come across as honest, aware, forthright and accessible.
3. Establish a reputation for availability and punctuality. If you receive a telephone call seeking to clarify points about your press release, jump to the matter. If further information is required send it immediately by fax, telex or courier.

Local radio

In some areas as many as two-thirds of a local population will listen to its independent or BBC local radio station at some point during any week. Such an important means of communication with the public should not be overlooked.

The standard of news required is often very much higher than in the case of the local or trade press. News can be restricted to only a few minutes every hour and national stories must be incorporated in such slots. For example, the opening of a new company in the locality could fail to prove sufficiently newsworthy in its own right. But if the opening involves specific major repercussions such as the creation of hundreds of new jobs in the area, then it is far more likely to be considered.

Local radio does, however, provide particularly good opportunities for the smaller business person in the following areas:

1. Involvement with charity or sponsorship.
2. Those with specialist knowledge.

    If you have specialist knowledge in a particular field it will undoubtedly be worth letting your radio station know. They might well get in touch to conduct an interview when they are planning to cover the subject in question. Such opportunities are likely to be greater on BBC local radio stations than independent ones because feature coverage tends to be greater.
3. Those with a story to tell.

    Radio is all about people talking, and those with a tale to tell are in demand. A businessman who has overcome notable restrictions to break into a new export market, for example, would stand a good chance of being interviewed, even though his story may not be news as such. Most radio stations would be happy to record such an interview over the telephone. In some circumstances they might even offer to come to your office.

Radio stations can be approached by news releases, but these should usually be kept even shorter than those sent to the press. Senders should also take greater care to be readily available for any follow-up questions. If they cannot be contacted on the same day that the material is intended for use their chances of success are limited. For those with a story to tell there is much to be said for making an initial enquiry by telephone. Newsrooms are invariably busy but most enquirers are likely to receive a sympathetic hearing.

If a story is good enough a local radio station may well pass it on to the national media. Local radio enjoys a strong relationship with national radio and – in the case of the BBC – even with television. This minimises the need for the smaller business person to concentrate his or her energies in these directions.

Points to remember

- Look out for opportunities for editorial in the local and trade press.
- Avoid submitting material to publications for which it isn't suitable.
- Never telephone to enquire whether a press release is going to be used.
- Do not enclose additional information with your press release.
- Try to develop long-term relationships with the press.

7
Obtaining Publicity Through Intermediaries

There are no set rules about whether or not a business should consider using an external organisation to obtain publicity. For those firms making the transition from being small to medium sized, however, the engagement of an agency to handle PR or advertising is often a logical step. It is one frequently taken when a specific act of expansion, such as the launching of a new range of products or the opening of new premises, has served as a springboard.

Those organisations that derive the bulk of their income from commission are called 'agencies' and those that operate mainly on a fee-paying basis are known as 'consultancies'. Although most organisations of both types have a core activity in which they specialise, there has been a distinct trend in the direction of providing a service in more than one field. An advertising agency is thus more than likely to be able to offer advice on direct mail and sales promotion; equally, a leading direct marketing agency may well have experience in conducting TV advertising campaigns. Some PR consultancies even handle their clients' advertising needs.

Many points specifically applicable to different types of agency and consultancy are outlined below. The following guidelines, however, apply almost universally.

Advantages of using agencies and consultancies

Agencies and consultancies are often able to provide levels of specialist knowledge vastly superior to those available in-house or which can be imported cost-effectively by further recruitment. They are usually well positioned to keep track of new developments in constantly changing market-places. Additionally, they are able to draw on a broad base of contacts.

They can save a company significant amounts of time by devising and executing entire campaigns. This can prove particularly useful for firms with a sporadic requirement. The agency can be used only when it is needed and the problems of having to carry surplus full-time staff to cater for one-off occasions are thus avoided.

Because agencies buy advertising space in bulk they receive commission from the media in return for their bookings. This is often refunded to their clients who can also enjoy significant further savings from the skill that is employed in media selection on their behalf.

Input

Many business people make the fundamental mistake of assuming that the only cost of employing an agency or consultancy lies in the fees and commissions that they pay out. If the relationship is to be effective the client company will have to put in considerable effort to ensure that the agency is fully conversant with its workings. The quality of work obtained from an agency will always depend to a large extent on the skill with which its staff have been briefed for a particular project and their degree of familiarity with the client's overall philosophy and approach.

If the partnership is to be truly successful the agency or consultancy should be treated as an extension of a company's own marketing department. This will necessitate frequent meetings. But there should be no need for you to leave your desk for the purpose of attending these. Most agencies should be willing to arrange meetings at your own premises at no extra cost. It is vital to establish that they are prepared to do so from the outset.

Basis of cooperation

All successful relationships between agency and client are based on a high degree of trust and informality. The exact terms and conditions under which the partnership is operating should, however, always be laid down in a formal written agreement. Systems of appraisal must be rigorously adhered to. Quotes and estimates should be obtained in writing. Copies of supplier invoices need to be requested to confirm the accuracy of expenses being charged. Most smaller business people would be well advised to take out contracts that are renewable annually. The advantage of sticking with the same agency for a long time cannot be overstressed. When an incorrect choice has clearly been made, however, the client should attempt to cut its losses as early as possible.

Size

Agencies and consultancies vary noticeably in size. Those which employ hundreds of staff will almost certainly derive the bulk of their business from multi-million pound organisations and are unlikely to show much interest in the smaller business. Most leading advertising agencies, for example, are rarely interested in taking on new clients with advertising budgets much below a quarter of a million pounds. On those occasions when they do, it will be because they can see that the company concerned has above average growth potential.

A small agency or consultancy can prove advantageous to a small business for a number of reasons. (See case study Russell and Bromley and Vernon Stratton Advertising, page 100.) There is always the possibility, however, that the quality of staff at a small agency may leave something to be desired. Growth in many marketing-related industries has been extremely rapid and suitably qualified recruits have not always been available. Particularly incompetent staff are likely to be weeded out more quickly than in the larger agencies. Exceptionally good staff, however, often fail to stay long at the smaller organisations because of not being able to obtain the rewards that their skills deserve.

Selection

Many of the sources from which agencies can be chosen are outlined below. A final decision should not be made until a shortlist has received due consideration. Obtain brochures from those you feel might be suitable and make preliminary enquiries by telephone to firms in which you develop a serious interest.

Once you have narrowed your selection down to three or four agencies which express obvious enthusiasm for your objectives and the size of budget you have available, prepare a detailed brief for each one outlining your plans in greater detail. Ask them to visit you to make a presentation, explaining how they would approach your intended projects and the terms and conditions under which they wish to operate. (Be prepared to pay them a briefing fee for doing this.) Try to ensure that more than one member of their staff come to visit you on such an occasion. Remember that staff are constantly moving on, so it is dangerous to base your opinion of an agency on the rapport that you strike with any one particular individual.

PR consultancies

PR consultancies are capable of doing considerably more than merely issuing press releases. Their activities can extend to designing videos, brochures and product literature, producing in-house magazines and newsletters, organising exhibitions and conferences, and identifying sponsorship and public speaking opportunities.

Press relations, however, invariably account for the bulk of a consultancy's activity. It can target press releases towards specific publications whose requirements have been closely scrutinised. Details of forthcoming features are obtained and clients' views developed accordingly. References to clients and competitors are monitored and industry trends detected. Most consultancies devote a great deal of time to developing long-term relationships with the press and their contacts will nearly always be significantly more numerous than those of an individual client company. They can arrange face-to-face meetings between clients and the press and, by closely monitoring the movements of key personnel, ensure that spokespersons are readily available to journalists seeking quotes over the phone.

Terms of remuneration can differ noticeably, not only from one consultancy to another but also among different clients represented by the same organisation. Some of the following elements are, however, commonly involved:

- A fixed retainer for counselling services;
- Additional fees directly related to time spent on the account in question;
- Additional administration expenses billed at cost;
- Further charges for work undertaken over and above the basic agreed programme.

Details of the majority of established PR consultancies, and useful advice on how to select the right one, can be obtained from *The Public Relations Yearbook* (£35, Financial Times Business Information). Those seeking advice on drawing up a shortlist of agencies should contact the Public Relations Consultants Association (PRCA) by telephoning 071-233 6026 or writing to:

PRCA
Willow House
Willow Place
London SW1P 1JH

The PRCA will send you details of its referral system which can help you to select a PR consultancy in your area. It will also enclose other useful information such as its free booklet 'Selecting and Employing a Public Relations Consultancy'. You complete and return the referral system form. The PRCA then puts this through its computer system and produces a brief list of suitable agencies for you to contact.

Advertising agencies

Operating through an advertising agency still carries with it many of the same problems faced when conducting in-house campaigns. Responses to individual advertisements are always likely to involve a high degree of volatility. Not even the most brilliant agency can say with any certainty that a particular item or campaign will prove successful.

Nevertheless, the costs of employing an advertising agency can often be repaid many times over by the results achieved. The benefits to the client can extend well beyond the creative expertise available for the design of his advertisements. An agency can ensure that advertisements conform to relevant codes of conduct, select the most suitable publications or other media forms in which to place them and arrange for the space itself to be booked. It may organise the printing of product literature, conduct market research and even handle a client's PR thrust. Some of the smaller agencies may use independent suppliers to fulfil many of these functions.

Traditionally, agencies have derived the bulk of their income from clients by charging a mark-up on the production work done on their behalf and commission for all the money spent on an advertising campaign – normally around 15 per cent. However, there is now a distinct trend towards charging a fee that reflects the value of advice given rather than its quantity.

Details of the vast majority of advertising agencies available can be obtained from *The Advertiser's Annual* – Volume 1 Agencies and Advertisers (£55, Reed Information S rvices). Those wishing to obtain free impartial advice on drawing up a shortlist of agencies can do so by writing in confidence to:

The Director General
The Institute of Practitioners in Advertising
44 Belgrave Square
London SW1X 8QS

Outline the type of agency you are looking for in a short letter. Explain the nature and size of your business and the geographical location(s) in which it operates. You will receive a shortlist of four suitable agencies.

Media independents

Media independents offer a ready alternative to an advertising agency for those who wish to conduct their planning and buying of media space through an external party. They are often able to provide a more personalised and less expensive service. The growth in popularity of media independents has been such that many new advertising agencies have elected to recommend them to their clients rather than set up their own media buying departments.

Confidential advice on selecting a suitable media independent can be obtained from:

The Director
The Association of Media Independents
34 Grand Avenue
London N10 3BP
Tel: 081-883 9854

Sales promotion consultancies

Any business considering launching competitions, incentives or other forms of sales promotion on a large scale would be well advised to consider the possibility of operating through a specialist consultancy. Most charge for their creative and conceptual services on a fee basis. This means that they are able to provide impartial advice with regard to which types of sales promotion are most suitable.

Sales promotion consultancies differ from advertising agencies in that they are often willing to consider being used on an *ad hoc* basis. Their services should thus not be ruled out by those embarking on a sizeable one-off promotion.

Details of the majority of established consultancies are available in the Institute of Sales Promotion (ISP) Consultants Register. This can be obtained free of charge by writing to:

The Secretary General
ISP Office
Arena House
66–68 Pentonville Road
London N1 9HS

Direct marketing agencies

The activities carried out by direct marketing agencies can embrace direct mail, telemarketing, off-the-page selling, poster design, database management and virtually any other method or technique relevant to direct response advertising. Details of most established agencies are listed in the British Direct Marketing Association (BDMA) *Handbook*. This can be obtained at a cost of £5 by writing to:

BDMA
Grosvenor Gardens House
Grosvenor Gardens
London SW1W 0BS

The BDMA also has a number of lists of names and addresses of approved agencies which specialise in particular aspects of direct marketing. They are available free of charge. Those wishing to seek out a telemarketing agency, for example, can obtain a list of 31 companies that operate in this field.

Case studies

Using an advertising agency

Russell and Bromley and Vernon Stratton Advertising
Few family businesses ever attain the size and stature of Russell and Bromley. It now operates through 43 shoe shops nationwide and employs over 1000 staff. Turnover is in the region of £50 million. But the company had to start from somewhere.

Its trading origins date back in one form or another to the opening of a single shop in Eastbourne in 1880. During the last quarter of a century it has trebled in size. The services of an advertising agency have played a major part in this expansion. 'In the 24 years since we have been with Vernon Stratton Advertising,' explains director Roger Bromley, 'we have made the change from being a big provincial shoe retailer to one of the leading national quality fashion retailers. Advertising has gone hand in hand with the development of the national image.'

It is most unusual for a company to strike such a lasting relationship with one particular agency. Compatibility in size has had much to do with this. Russell and Bromley has always been small in comparison with other national shoe retailers. Vernon Stratton Advertising, meanwhile, employs only about 20 staff.

Mr Roger Bromley is in little doubt of the advantages that have resulted from sticking with the same small agency. 'We enjoy the personal contact of the Strattons,' he explains. 'They know what we want and what we don't want and are able to sense opportunities on our behalf. This doesn't happen if you change agencies.'

'The main advantage of a small agency is that the people running it are very close to their business,' he continues. 'A bad account executive is therefore unlikely to last long. I'm sure that if Vernon thought that something was going wrong he would phone up. They are probably not aggressive enough but we don't really need aggression.'

The main thrust of Russell and Bromley's advertising centres around promoting five styles of ladies' shoes in a range of fashion magazines. TV is considered too expensive and radio unsuitable for the purposes of selling fashion. The advertising year is split into two seasons. When a forthcoming campaign is being considered the results from the previous season are analysed. 'If we like what we are doing then we basically do it again with knobs on,' explains Roger Bromley. 'We have evolved a number of appearances and we plus or minus these depending on how we feel about a season and increase the budget to cater for inflation.'

Such considerations appear straightforward enough at first glance. Indeed, one might well be tempted to wonder why they require the services of an advertising agent at all. The contribution made by Vernon Stratton Advertising has, however, proved important for a large number of reasons.

1. Media selection
'They convinced us of the need to put our resources into the right media,' explains Roger Bromley. 'If we hadn't had their advice we would have probably used the press too much instead of concentrating on full page colour spreads in the full spectrum of fashion magazines.' The world of fashion magazines is constantly chopping and changing so the agency's expertise in media selection is also important on an ongoing basis. The company relies on it to recommend whether or not it should carry on advertising in a particular publication.

2. Advertisement design
Photographic sessions require a high degree of coordination as well as skill. Shoes must be seen on people's feet and fashion shoes must appear in the right context. Men and women models are involved.

3. Added dimensions
On a number of occasions the relationship with Vernon Stratton Advertising has led to projects being carried out that would not otherwise have been considered. A move into handbag advertising, for example, resulted from Mr Vernon Stratton being approached on a basis of 'the will is there if you can come up with the adverts'. Mr Stratton has also been responsible for redesigning the company's logo. The ideas involved occurred over a long period. Russell and Bromley had decided that a design consultancy would not be approached for the purpose, but that changes would be made if the agency proved capable of suitable suggestions.

4. Objective advice
Russell and Bromley does all its PR in-house. No external organisation other than Vernon Stratton Advertising is involved with its marketing or advertising strategy. The objective advice that the agency is able to provide on all aspects of its affairs is thus highly valued. 'It is very useful having someone who is not on the payroll telling us what they think from a professional point of view,' explains Roger Bromley. 'If we were going wrong I'm sure Vernon would tell us.'

Communication between the two parties involves its fair share of formal meetings. These fall into two basic categories. Media meetings examine the various alternative forms of media intended for use. Actual advertisement design and content are discussed at a subsequent gathering. Roger Bromley confesses that both he and other members of his staff do actually leave their desks to attend such occasions at the agency's Ives Street premises in London, but he stresses that it is not essential for them to do so. If necessary all meetings could be conducted at Russell and Bromley's own headquarters in Bromley, Kent.

The advantages that have resulted from such an effective partnership have clearly been considerable. Nevertheless, Roger Bromley points to the fact that there is no yardstick by which one can measure when a company should start to consider using an agency. Indeed, he emphasises that there are many cases when it might not be suitable to use an agency or even to advertise at all. Some of his leading competitors in retail shoes do not in fact do any advertising.

'If you've got the wrong goods then advertising won't sell them for you,' maintains Mr Bromley, 'and if you've got a good product then it will sell itself. If, however, you match the right advertisement with the right product at the right time then you do the product a service because you sell more. You also do your company profile a tremendous amount of good.' He sees the practice of advertising as providing further valuable side effects. 'If you advertise you must decide what you are, who you are and what you stand for. This is a good regulator for people in a small to medium-sized business.'

Using a public relations (PR) consultancy

Emstar and Good Relations

Emstar provides a range of professional energy management services. Contract Energy Management, the core business activity, offers a comprehensive and flexible way for energy needs to be managed by an outside party. The company is a subsidiary of Shell, but operates very much as an autonomous unit. It employs 180 staff. Turnover is in the region of £30 million.

Emstar now works in conjunction with some 200 blue chip companies and leading public sector organisations. Growth has, however, been extremely rapid. Only 20 staff were employed when it was launched in 1984. At that time few organisations had ever heard of the concept of energy management. The initial challenge was twofold: awareness had to be built both of the company itself and of the new industry and concept which was involved. An extensive public relations campaign was considered essential and the cooperation of Good Relations, a leading London PR consultancy, was obtained.

The publicity that Good Relations has generated has played a major part in enabling Emstar to maintain its position in a competitive market-place. 'I'm not sure we could have ever really got off the ground without PR,' explains Dr David Strong, Sales and Marketing Director. 'It has done much to increase the general level of awareness of what we do. I am constantly meeting people at exhibitions and other gatherings who refer to articles they have seen. Some of our competitors have failed to grow as effectively as a result of not exploiting PR.' Dr Strong points to successes that the consultancy has initiated in the following areas.

Press relations
Many of the messages that have needed to be imparted are highly complex. The markets they have been aimed at have meanwhile been highly diverse and subject to constantly changing environmental conditions. 'If you look at what you would have had to generate in-house it is not difficult to see that you are getting value for money by using an outside party,' explains Dr Strong, 'especially when you consider that you often need three or four people for a short period only. Even if we had our own in-house PR team it still wouldn't have the breadth of contacts enjoyed by Good Relations.'

The essential thrust of the press relations campaign has been to clearly establish Emstar as problem-solvers and professional partners. Views on industry, environmental issues and news of specific launches and contract signings have presented particular opportunities. The signing of a £50 million contract with Tunnel Refineries for a major combined heat and power scheme, for example, led to some 40 major pieces of press coverage. Many of these were entire feature length articles. (An example of a detailed press release used in the campaign is provided on page 108.)

'I can't say that any particular contract came as a result,' explains Dr Strong, 'but the campaign certainly helped to establish us as an industry leader.'

Brochures and newsletters
Good Relations produce a regular half-yearly newsletter for their clients entitled 'Energy Matters'. This is aimed at existing and

potential clients as well as other external contacts and influences. Interest in the newsletter has been such that a number of trade journals have actually asked for permission to reproduce articles from it.

The consultancy has also been involved with designing Emstar's leaflets and brochures. It is asked to tender work of this nature along with other parties. The fact that it already has an extensive knowledge of the company's affairs, however, means that it enjoys a clear advantage in terms of the time needed for such tasks to be performed. As a result it is often able to quote competitively. Emstar agrees a fee with Good Relations at the beginning of each year for a set scope of work. Payment is made quarterly. When additional one-off projects crop up, however, they are invoiced separately.

'PR is a two-way phenomenon,' stresses Dr Strong, 'and a company has to put in a fair amount of effort if it is to make effective use of its agency. We believe it is important to have monthly meetings and we see the account managers and directors we deal with as being members of one of our teams. You must have that sort of relationship for it to work.' Such events are normally attended by two or three representatives from both parties. The previous month's activities are reviewed, press cuttings are presented and forthcoming features discussed. The locations of the meetings tend to be spread fairly evenly between the two parties' respective premises. If necessary, however, all could be held at Emstar's own headquarters in Staines without any extra charge being made.

Emstar conducts annual reviews of the contribution that Good Relations is making. 'You must always be looking to see that you are getting the right service,' explains Dr Strong. 'After several years a lack of fresh ideas or complacency must be clearly guarded against, however competent the organisation you are dealing with. A further point that must be watched out for is the fact that PR agencies are made up of groups of people. If staff who have given you continuity leave it can have the same effect as changing agency and can be highly disruptive. The small print of an agency's contract should also be carefully examined, in particular notice periods and penalty payments in the event of early termination of the contract.'

Emstar Press Information

Contract Energy Management

Issued by
Good Relations Limited
59 Russell Square
London WC1B 4HJ

Tel: 01-631 3434
Telex: 265903
Fax: 01-631 1399

Date: 31 July 1989
Contact: Catherine Perry   Tel: 01-631 3434

MONKEY BUSINESS AT LONDON ZOO

Apes, elephants, giraffes and storks are a few of the new
clients recently acquired by Emstar Ltd, Shell UK's Contract
Energy Management company.

London Zoo has formed a partnership with Emstar where the
welfare of the animals in the Zoo is of prime importance.
With energy bills that amount to £400,000 a year, the Zoo
could not afford to replace its old boilers and heating
systems in order to provide the best environment for the
animals. As a result, Emstar has invested £420,000 in new
energy efficient heating and hot water systems and has taken
on the responsibility for its day-to-day management.

Using its expertise in energy management, Emstar has taken
into account the fact that each house within the Zoo has its
own independent energy needs and many of the inhabitants
need to be individually catered for. As a result, under its
10 year contract Emstar has decentralised the main
boilerhouse and installed new localised boilers in 14 boiler
rooms. It has also provided heating zones and individual
time and temperature controls, and extensive new heating
systems.

The benefits to the animals are far-reaching. Now that the
animal houses have their own individual boilers it is easier
to maintain a temperature to suit a particular creature's

Emstar Limited, Elizabeth House, 56/60 London Road, Staines, Middlesex TW18 4BQ Tel: 0784 458431
○ A member of the Royal Dutch Shell Group of Companies

needs. The Zoo requires a flexible system to cope with the warmer conditions needed for the multitude of births that occur every year. Under the old system it would have been very difficult to supply two animal houses with different heating levels which also vary at certain times of the day. The new energy system enables this to be achieved thus providing essential environmental improvements.

Emstar has provided a complete service including finance, engineering expertise and a monitoring service which puts the welfare of the animals first. The financial gains made from the savings are a secondary consideration although the savings made on fuel consumption will provide additional finance for the Zoo and the capital that would have needed to be invested can be directed elsewhere.

For further information:
Catherine Perry
Good Relations Ltd
59 Russell Square
London WC1B 4HJ   Tel: 01-631 3434

Emstar Press Information

Issued by
Good Relations Limited
59 Russell Square
London WC1B 4HJ

Tel: 01-631 3434
Telex: 265903
Fax: 01-631 1399

Date: 8 August 1989
Contact: Georgina Asprey. 01-631 3434

EMSTAR LEADS THE WAY WITH £50 MILLION CHP CONTRACT WITH TUNNEL REFINERIES

Tunnel Refineries Limited, manufacturers of glucose syrups and starches, part of CST/Tate & Lyle Group, has signed a £50 million contract with Emstar Ltd, the subsidiary of Shell UK Limited, to install and operate a new combined heat and power (CHP) plant at its Greenwich refinery.

The ten year contract, involving a capital investment by Emstar of some £8.0 million, and providing energy services over the contract period to the value of £50 million, is a landmark in the development of large scale CHP schemes. It is the largest contract in the UK to be engineered, funded and operated by a Contract Energy Management company and involves the generation of nearly 15 MW of electricity.

The imminent privatisation of electricity and anticipated increases in electricity prices, combined with falling gas and oil prices make CHP schemes increasingly attractive for large industrial energy users. Quite apart from reducing their annual energy bill, Tunnel expect the new plant to improve the security of their electricity supply to the site, reducing the risk of costly production shutdowns.

- more -

Emstar Limited, Elizabeth House, 56/60 London Road, Staines, Middlesex TW18 4BQ Tel: 0784 458431
A member of the Royal Dutch Shell Group of Companies

The contract with Emstar will not only enable Tunnel to
generate enough electricity and steam to satisfy all of its
own requirements but will at times create a surplus of
electricity which will be made available for export to the
London Electricity Board.

At the same time the contract will provide for a net
reduction in Tunnel's current energy bill of an estimated
10% per annum - a projected saving of around £500,000 p.a.

The contract involves the installation of new combined heat
and power plant comprising two 6MW(e) gas turbine
electricity generators linked to two new waste heat boilers.
The new plant will work in conjunction with an existing
2.2MW(e) steam turbine driven electricity generator.

The existing boiler plant will be retained to serve as
standby to the new plant, and electricity will be imported
from the LEB in the event of breakdown or during maintenance
of the new CHP plant.

The contract also includes provision of other new ancillary
plant in the Power House Complex such as a new water
treatment plant, water storage tanks and motor control
centres.

Emstar will be providing all the necessary engineering and
project management expertise to install all the new plant
and equipment and will be retained thereafter to take sole
responsibility for its operation and maintenance. Thus, all
of the utility services - electricity, steam, demineralised
water, soft water, and compressed air required for the
Tunnel production process will be supplied from the Central
Power House operated by Emstar.

- more -

Hugh Fox, Managing Director of Tunnel Refineries commented:

"Companies such as Tunnel Refineries in the UK have become
increasingly concerned about the cost of electricity,
especially in comparison to similar industries on the
Continent of Europe. It is therefore becoming more
attractive for large users such as Tunnel to generate their
own electricity.

"Tunnel Refineries selected Emstar for the job because we
did not want to use scarce in house engineering and
financial resources for the development of a CHP project
when their expertise was readily available on an extremely
competitive basis. The £8 million capital expenditure
required for this project has been funded by Emstar. This
in turn allows us to release capital for investment in
mainstream production processes."

John Ashcroft, Emstar's Managing Director said "Since Emstar
was launched by the Secretary of State for Energy in 1984 we
have established ourselves as the UK's leading energy
management company. We provide our clients with the
finance, engineering and project management expertise
as well as the operating skills required to upgrade and
manage their organisations' energy services. We have
developed a particular expertise in the engineering and
operation of CHP plants and feel sure that the Tunnel
project will become a model for others to follow".

ENDS

For further information please contact:

Georgina Asprey
Good Relations Limited
59 Russell Square
London WC1B 4HJ

Tel. 01-631 3434

Using a direct marketing agency

Design Marketing and WWAV

Design Marketing is a small business which promotes a range of different marketing projects from its offices in Andover. It employs only 20 staff and has a turnover in the region of £5 million. Many of its products are sold through in-house mail order operations. In 1987, however, it devised a scheme for selling limited editions of fine art prints. The service of a direct marketing agency were considered necessary if the idea was to be developed to its full potential.

Finding a shortlist of suitable agencies was never going to be easy. The budget available for a trial campaign was only £50,000. 'We found that when contacting the larger agencies you almost get asked what your budget is by the switchboard operator,' explains chairman Brian Rogers. Interest was sufficient, however, for the initial pitch to be contested between three agencies, all of whom showed considerable enthusiasm.

The successful candidate was Watson Ward Albert Varndell (WWAV), the UK's largest direct marketing agency. The two others had offered to provide large quantities of inserts. WWAV's approach was noticeably different. It suggested a double page spread in the *Mail on Sunday* colour supplement. A single print was to be offered on a send no money basis with an invoice and a catalogue giving details of the other prints available in the series.

Response to the advertisement was better than originally anticipated and further bookings were made in a range of other colour supplements. It was soon clear that the most suitable approach to promoting the product to first-time buyers had been found. The advertisements were expensive. Some cost as much as £30,000 each. The response generated was, however, more cost-effective than that which could have been achieved through large-scale direct mail campaigns.

Direct mail, nevertheless, plays an important part in the operation's profitability. It is used to inform those who have already bought of new opportunities. 'If we only sell one print to the original person then we lose money,' explains Mr Rogers. Each time a new series of prints is devised the procedure is thus twofold. Advertisements are placed to attract new customers and mail-shots are sent to existing customers.

'Throughout the campaign the company has hardly ever lifted a finger without consulting WWAV,' enthuses Mr Rogers.

'Without its cooperation the project would not have gone ahead. It would have been far too expensive to have attempted to have replaced WWAV's expertise by taking on additional members of staff.' He highlights the following areas of contribution.

Advertisements
'With some of our other products it is feasible to organise our own in-house mailings because you don't need the same degree of creative expertise,' explains Mr Rogers. 'If you are going to spend £30,000 on an advertisement, however, you might as well get it right.' WWAV has not only designed all the advertisements involved, it has also booked them through its media department. Mr Rogers acknowledges that space booking can be done in-house but points to WWAV's far superior skill in selecting the right opportunities.

Follow-up literature
WWAV has designed and organised the production of the letters, brochures and other follow-up literature right up to the stage of placing them in envelopes and putting them in the post. Some mailings have involved as many as 40,000 letters. The agency provides advice on the cost-effectiveness of the response that is achieved. It could even have assumed responsibility for the handling of replies through its own fulfilment house but Design Marketing preferred to deal with these directly.

Large-scale campaign
Not all editions of prints have proved profitable in their own right and individual advertisements have achieved markedly different responses. In some newspapers response can be five or ten times greater or smaller in one week than in another. The ability to conduct a prolonged large-scale campaign has done much to offset the problems caused by such peaks and troughs. Because the services of an agency have been available no more than three of Design Marketing's staff (including Mr Rogers himself) have needed to be involved with the project.

Points to remember

- Agencies receive commission from the media for bulk space buying.
- An agency will normally have an extensive range of contacts.

- Agencies can be highly suitable for those with sporadic requirements.
- A client company must put in a considerable amount of effort.
- There should be no need for you to leave your desk to attend meetings.
- Always select agencies from a shortlist.
- Try to meet more than one member of staff of the agencies being considered.
- Some associations offer free advice on drawing up shortlists.
- Agencies can provide useful objective advice on overall strategy.
- An agency's contribution must be continually assessed.

8
Equipping the Office

The equipment in an office can play a major part in enhancing productivity. It can greatly increase the speed of decision-making and provide valuable contact with the outside world. Technological advance has ensured that there is now no shortage of sophisticated systems well within the budget of even the smallest business. However, the task of deciding what equipment is necessary, and which models are most suitable, is not an easy one.

A wealth of information is available. For the complete beginner the contents of most specialised publications are likely to be too detailed and will provide as much confusion as they will knowledge. The novice would be better advised to read more general articles on the subject. Office equipment and information technology have now become such an essential part of business that many trade and professional publications provide occasional overviews of the market.

If you do not subscribe regularly to a magazine in this subject area you would be well advised to do so. The pace of technological change is such that new developments are constantly occurring. A quarterly publication such as *Managing Your Business* (Keymark Communications, £12.00 per annum) will provide you with information on any major changes in this field, as well as in most other areas of interest to those managing a small business.

Selecting the right furniture

Sitting all day at the wrong kind of desk can constitute a gross mismanagement of resources. It can make organisation and filing difficult and have a detrimental effect on morale. Most business people think nothing of devoting considerable time and energy to selecting a suitable secretary because they know they will have to spend the greater part of their working lives with her or him. They do not, however, view the choice of desk in the same light, despite the fact that they will spend more hours at their desk than with their secretary.

The choice of the right desk should be considered a subject of major importance. Great attention should also be paid to other office furniture. Making the right selection can enhance productivity by effective use of space, adding to the attractiveness of a working environment and creating a favourable impression on visitors. Design your work area to avoid unnecessary movement, so that the most frequently used files etc are to hand when the phone rings.

Attitudes to office furniture and work areas have changed noticeably during the last few years. Rapidly rising office rents and rates have dictated that space cannot be wasted and new technology has created the need for sophisticated machinery to be accommodated.

Good quality furniture can last for a generation, but there is always the danger that your requirements will change during its useful life. If, for example, you opt for ultra-modern designs they may well become out of date and need to be replaced, so there is much to be said for being conservative in your tastes. It is also wise to ensure that your furniture is adaptable. Should you expand your premises or move to a new address, your needs could well change.

Always check that the manufacturer intends to continue production of your chosen style so that you will be able to make future additions. Use a company that includes in its price a free survey of the storage and filing purposes to be catered for and make sure that it offers an after-sales service. Allow plenty of time for delivery: three months is not uncommon. If you are in a particular hurry select a firm that holds substantial stocks.

There are as many as 700 furniture manufacturers and each company's representatives are inevitably intent on pushing their own products as strongly as possible. The one body in the UK which offers completely independent and impartial advice on the choice of furniture is the Office Furniture Advisory Service (OFAS). The annual membership fee is £90 plus VAT. Members are entitled to as many consultations by telephone or letter as they require at no further charge. Each query is dealt with individually within 24 hours. Where an in-depth survey is needed a representative will be sent to visit a member on site for a mutually agreed additional fee. OFAS can be contacted at:

OFAS
Suite B
Manhattan House
140 High Street
Crowthorne
Berkshire RG11 7AT
Tel: 0344 779438

Personal computers

After its personnel, information is arguably the most important resource of any business. The widespread availability of affordable computerisation has thus made a major impression on current business practices, and the number of offices that can actually afford to be without a computer is becoming increasingly small. We have already established that time should be viewed in the same way as money. Any equipment that will save large quantities of time is therefore likely to make a substantial contribution to profitability in the long run.

Desktop personal computers can perform a wide range of functions. They are capable of handling accounting, filing, project planning, word processing (see below), stock control, research analysis and virtually any task that involves dealing with large quantities of information. A suitably programmed personal computer can, in fact, improve your record-keeping to the extent of enabling you to obtain vital information during a telephone conversation by merely pressing a few switches.

IBM continues to dominate the market for low priced personal computers. Amstrad, Apple, Compaq and Olivetti are among the other companies that have made major inroads into the sector. For those seeking a good general purpose model the IBM Personal System/2 range is particularly worthy of note. It is simple to use, fast working and highly versatile. It is suitable for both a small company planning to introduce computers and for a large one wishing to extend the scope of its existing applications.

There is, however, a huge number of different models on the market and each business would be well advised to give due consideration to selecting the system which most closely matches its own requirements. Making the wrong decision could prove catastrophic. It is far better not to have a computer at all than to obtain an unsuitable one. An incorrect choice is likely to cost considerably more than just the purchase price. If you find that after months of feeding in information the system fails to provide the service you require, you will have wasted a great deal of time and money.

By all means listen to recommendations from friends and colleagues but do not consider them as more than a guide. Few people are willing to admit that they have spent thousands of pounds on something that they shouldn't have bought in the first place. Furthermore, even if a system is working well for someone else it may not be the one for your office.

The first step in selecting a computer is to identify clearly what functions you intend it to perform and what you will be providing in the way of input. Customer information can be stored so as to provide relevant lists of prospects for specific items or campaigns. Sales input can be analysed by size of customer, size of orders, geographical area and type of business. Stock levels can be automatically adjusted as invoices and credit notes are processed.

You should then ask a number of different suppliers to provide you with information and quotations on systems that match your requirements. Once you have established a shortlist of those models that appear most suitable, arrange for the companies concerned to give a demonstration in your office.

Those who require completely impartial advice on their computing affairs should contact the Association of Professional Computer Consultants (APCC) (tel: 081-422 6460). It is the only professional association in Europe solely for advisers and experts in information technology who are both experienced and demonstrably independent. It can arrange for a consultant to visit you to provide impartial advice on your computer requirements. The fee charged for this service is likely to be several hundred pounds per day. In many cases, however, such an outlay could constitute a highly worthwhile investment. Consultants can be chosen from details provided by the APCC.

Telecommunications

Most business people take the presence of their existing telephone arrangements for granted. They do not consider whether the system has become out of date or in need of replacement as they do with photocopiers and other standard items of office equipment. This could be reducing efficiency, as the field of telecommunications is a highly technical and rapidly changing area.

It is usually more expensive to carry on using a telephone system when you have outgrown its capacity than to invest in a new one with a slightly greater capacity than you actually need. If, for example, you have an inadequate number of exchange lines it could mean that customers who are attempting to call you find that your lines are blocked. This in turn is likely to have a directly detrimental effect on the number of sales you make. If you note the number of calls which your business makes and receives during the busiest part of the day, you can then discuss with potential suppliers how many exchange lines you need.

Exchanges and systems

All exchange lines must be rented from one of the three public telecommunications operators: British Telecom, Mercury Communications or (for those who live in the Hull area) Kingston Communications. British Telecom still accounts for well over 90 per cent of the market. However, the competition that Mercury has been providing has grown steadily. It has two main services specifically designed for the business user. These are the Mercury 2100 – directly connected – and Mercury 2200 – indirectly connected.

The principal attractions these have over British Telecom are to be found in lower call charges. Local calls (only available on the directly connected service) are on average 16 per cent cheaper. Because charges are made by the second (after a minimum charge of three pence) customers pay only for the exact time used rather than for an entire unit – as is the case with British Telecom services. The provision of free itemised billing also represents a major selling point. The itemised bills range from summaries listing the total number of calls made to a specific place to highly detailed reports giving the length, destination, time and cost of every single call. Cost centre codes, which enable call charges to be allocated to particular accounts, are a further option. These can help you to work out how much you are actually spending on a particular client and whether this is justified by the amount of business you are receiving from him or her.

While your exchange line must be rented from a public telephone operator, the apparatus that you connect to it can be bought, rented or leased from a wide range of sources. The Office of Telecommunications (OFTEL) issues a number of useful guides to help you to make the right choices. These include a free and regularly updated list of published sources of information on UK suppliers and apparatus. Details can be obtained by contacting:

OFTEL Library
Atlantic House
Holborn Viaduct
London EC1N 2HQ
Tel: 071-822 1665

Should you require further advice contact a telecommunications consultant. You should find details of those in your area from Yellow Pages or your Thomson Local Directory. Alternatively, your local Chamber of Commerce may be able to put you in touch with one. (Many of the telephone devices that can directly increase your sales are described in Chapter 4.)

Transmitting information

Telephone networks provide more than a means of merely making a telephone call. Other methods of communication such as telex, E-mail (electronic mail) and fax (facsimile) rely on its use to transmit texts and images electronically. For those who spend all day at their desks these provide a useful extra dimension of communication with other businesses and even separate branches of their own organisation. The presence of at least one such system can save valuable time as well as offering ready solutions to emergencies.

One of the most important criteria for deciding which of these systems to select concerns the extent to which each is used by your major clients, suppliers and distributors. Some systems are used more widely in particular trades and industries than others. You may find that your trade association is able to provide you with useful guidelines on the subject.

Telex

The telex continues to be one of the most economical methods of sending brief urgent messages. Its use, however, is governed by certain notable restrictions. It cannot be employed for sending plans or diagrams and its vocabulary permits only the use of capital letters and limited punctuation. Furthermore, a separate telex line must be rented. You cannot use your existing telephone line for transmitting or receiving.

Modern telexes usually have their own word processing facilities so that messages can be easily composed and edited before being transmitted. They also often have memory banks which enable users to feed in their own business directories of most frequently used telex numbers. The machine is then automatically programmed to dial the required number. Some machines will keep trying an engaged telex number until they get an answer, or will alert the user if they have been unable to transmit a message after a certain period.

It is, in fact, not necessary to acquire a telex machine as such. There are various economical devices available which can be added on to an office or personal computer. Telex boxes, as they are called, can allow you to send and receive telexes without preventing the computer from performing other functions at the same time.

If your business has only a limited demand for a telex you may be better advised to use a telex bureau such as British Telecom's Text Direct or Mercury's Link 7500. You dictate your message over the phone and the bureau transmits it for you via its own machine. Incoming messages are sent to you over the phone followed by paper copies through the post. You can also send or receive messages from a telex bureau through direct microcomputer links.

Sales letters can be sent by telex instead of direct mail through the post. However, they may prevent your prospect receiving an urgent message and use up the paper supply on his or her machine, so tread warily. Similar problems apply to sending sales letters by fax. Do not antagonise a potential customer.

Facsimile (fax)

A fax service has a clear superiority over rival forms of communication in that it allows you to transmit entire documents in a photocopied format. This means that you can send drawings, diagrams, graphs and other illustrations as well as merely text and figures. It can be used on the same line as your telephone but, if you wish to be able to use both your telephone and fax machine at the same time, you will need an additional line.

Fax machines are simple to operate. You place the document you wish to send into a slot on the side or front of your machine, dial the fax number of the intended recipient and when this responds press a transit button. The document will then be reproduced at the other end. Regular maintenance is, however, invariably necessary. It is therefore a good idea to take out a contract for this at the outset.

Most machines available for purchase or lease are Group 3 types. They are able to transmit an A4 size sheet of paper in under one minute. Speed of transmission is, however, governed by the rate at which the receiving fax is able to operate and by the quality of lines available over the public switched telephone network. The latter will gradually improve as all the public networks become digital. In the mean time those businesses which make above average use of their fax machines should consider leasing special lines on the public data network over which optimum performance can be obtained.

There are well over 100 different types of fax machine to choose from. Prices have been on a downward trend and some models are now available for between £500 and £1000. British Telecom, Betacom and Brother are among the major forces at the low cost end of the market.

If you do not wish to obtain your own fax machine but need to send short documents from time to time you can take advantage of a public fax service. British Telecom's Bureaufax and the Post Office's Intel Post are examples of services which can be accessed from a microcomputer or modem.

Most mail order shots now include a fax number so customers can place an order immediately, transmitting the coupon, filled in with details of the order, name and address of sender and – most important – the credit card to be debited. The fax can be left on while the office is closed, and you arrive to a pile of orders in the morning!

Electronic mail (E-mail)

E-mail is the general title given to a collection of different services which enable users of personal or office computers to send and receive messages and have information stored for them on a central computer by a service provider. The leading organisations in the UK at the moment are Telecom Gold, One-To-One and Mercury Link 7500.

Most services operate along broadly the same lines. You pay a basic registration fee to the E-mail provider. You are then allocated a 'mailbox identity code' on which a monthly rental or minimum invoice is charged. To send or receive messages from other users of the service you need a computer terminal or a microcomputer equipped to act as a terminal.

All messages are sent and received via a central computer system run by the service provider. To send a message to another mailbox you contact the central computer by dialling a special telephone number, then transmit a message to the relevant mailbox code. This is stored and can only be seen by the recipient once he or she has unlocked his or her mailbox by connecting to the computer and giving a private password. The same procedure applies in reverse. Every time you dial into the computer you receive a brief message informing you whether there is any mail for you. This can only be retrieved when you have entered your own private password.

Unlike telex, E-mail allows you to use all the characters found on a normal typewriter or word processor keyboard – and even more in addition. The disadvantage that E-mail shares with telex, however, is that it cannot be used for transmitting pictures or diagrams. Furthermore, unlike telex, there is the inconvenience of having to dial the service's computer to find out whether it has any messages stored for you.

Mailing equipment

Word processors

Those who are still unfamiliar with the advantages of using a word processor as opposed to a typewriter would be well advised to investigate the matter. It can make a fundamental difference to a business's mailing efficiency in terms of both speed and quality. For those indulging in direct mail activities (described in Chapter 3) it is an essential tool in all but the very smallest of campaigns.

A word processor offers the distinct advantage of having separate typing and printing functions. Text is entered from a keyboard on to a display screen where it can be edited. This greatly reduces the problems caused by initial typing errors and enables the same piece of text to be adapted to suit different circumstances. If, for example, you are sending a circular letter all you need to do is enter a new name and address on each one. Furthermore, text can be stored in a disk for future reference or for printing at a later date. Basic word processors which are simple to use can now be obtained for around £500. Amstrad is the major company at the bottom end of the market.

Franking machines

Any office that sends sizeable quantities of mail should seriously consider whether it is worth acquiring a franking machine. It will stamp the amount of postage required on to your envelopes and measure your liability for postal charges in a meter. Such a machine can spare the discomfort of licking huge quantities of stamps and save a considerable amount of time. Many versions offer additional facilities such as automatic envelope feeders, sealers and tape dispensers.

Franked mail has the advantage over postage stamps on

grounds of more than just speed and convenience. It short-cuts important sorting processes at the Post Office, giving mail the chance of catching earlier despatches. A business can also benefit substantially from valuable prestige and free advertising as the company name or a message/slogan can be overprinted on each envelope by means of a slub (which is changeable).

One of the traditional drawbacks of a franking machine used to be that you had to carry the meter to the Post Office at frequent intervals and wait around to have it recredited. Modern technology now ensures that it is no longer necessary to leave your desk for such a purpose. Franking companies have started to produce models which enable your meter to be recredited automatically from your office.

Franking machines, however, are not without their drawbacks:

- Company funds are frozen in the meter and the cost of leasing or purchase is also a major consideration.
- The very cheapest models on the market sell for around £600 and the more sophisticated versions cost several thousand pounds.
- The reputations of some of the salesforces concerned have at times tended to leave something to be desired.
- There are currently only six companies in the franking machine market. Pitney Bowes and Alcatel Business Systems have the lion's share of the business. Hasler is third in volume terms. Envopak, Cheshire Mailing and Addressing Systems International are the smaller players.
- If the machine goes wrong, mail despatch is held up until it is serviced.
- There is some evidence that franked letters move more slowly than others through the mail system.

Other mailing equipment

The mailroom has been proving a boom area for office equipment suppliers, and a particular trend towards producing items that sit comfortably in the small office has become evident. Automatic labellers and addressing machines are in abundant supply. Electronic postal scales, letter openers, folding machines, and numerous other forms of equipment are also widely available. Innovation has been such that virtually every need is now catered for. Some devices even verge on the side of the eccentric. Those who find writing their name an undue strain can, for example, obtain an automatic cheque signer.

Of those multi-purpose systems suitable for a business with a small mailing requirement the Pitney Bowes 3285 desktop folder/inserter/sealer is particularly worthy of note. It is the smallest desktop inserter available worldwide and, at up to 1500 cycles per hour, is the fastest machine of its type. It will automatically fold paper of varying size and weight in either a single, double or standard format. It can insert up to two separate items into most types of envelope and seal them ready for franking.

Alcatel's System 7 is also suitable for a small office. It provides an automatic flexible mailing system to handle invoices, sales letters, daily mail and numerous other requirements. Feeding, collating, folding, inserting and sealing are all available in one non-stop operation. The system can be easily expanded by the installation of additional units. Prominent among its many special features is its ability to sense the thickness and therefore the weight of filled envelopes and to select them automatically according to the relevant postal rates. Mail within the standard letter rate is directed through one of the exits to a linked franking machine. The heavier mail is ejected from the other exit and is stacked for separate attention.

Points to remember

- Subscribe to a publication which provides regular updates on technology.
- Choosing a suitable desk is essential if you are never to leave it.
- Selecting the wrong computer could prove catastrophic.
- An inadequate telephone system can have a detrimental effect on sales.
- Establish whether your main sources of contact use fax, telex or E-mail.
- Word processing is essential for conducting mailing campaigns.
- Some franking machines can be recredited without leaving your desk.
- Mailing equipment is now available to cater for virtually any need.

9
Getting the Best Out of Other People

There are few set rules about how staff can be motivated effectively. In a small business there tend to be even fewer than elsewhere. This is because many of the standard guidelines which apply to meetings, group training sessions and other occasions that go hand in hand with large-scale resources and staff numbers have only limited relevance. Whatever the size of the firm, however, one fundamental rule applies. Those who are able to get other people to do things are usually worth far more to an organisation than those who merely attain a high standard of proficiency in their own roles.

There is no doubt that some people are born with a considerably greater aptitude for leadership than others. A natural ability to make decisions and to communicate is certainly hard to rival. Even those who fail by substantial margins to qualify as born leaders can, however, do much to enhance their propensity to influence others by making a conscious effort. Attention to the following areas can help to improve the extent to which other people increase your sales without your having to leave your desk.

Showing interest

No matter what level of interest your staff demonstrate or pretend to in your company you can rest assured that they will always be more interested in themselves than in anything else. People are essentially selfish. Once this fundamental point has been understood it can be readily exploited. Try to make people feel important. Show a genuine interest in the duties they perform and call them by their first names at every opportunity.

Never forget that effective communication is a two-way phenomenon. The ability to listen to what other people have to say is just as important as being able to speak clearly yourself. Indeed, those who are exceptionally articulate are often among the very worst communicators on a day-to-day basis. This is because they are invariably engrossed in the pastime of listening to their own voices. Other people's opinions must be given due respect even on those occasions when they are clearly ill- informed or wrong. This can require considerable patience.

Try to look people straight in the eye when you are talking to them and avoid creating distractions through awkward mannerisms. Keep your hands still. It is important that you fully understand what people are trying to say. Avoid interrupting; but once they have finished speaking do not be afraid to summarise their main points in your own words.

Honesty

Any policy of dealing with staff must be based on total honesty. Attempts at sharp practice are almost bound to be counter-productive. Few things travel faster than gossip among a workforce. People will never judge your company on the way that it has treated them alone. They are always keen to know how other people are being dealt with as well. An injustice suffered by a single member of staff could thus lead to an atmosphere of mistrust in a working environment for several years. Promotion that appears to be based on favouritism as opposed to merit can prove a particular source of grievance. For many people the prospect of being promoted is a principal motivating factor. Their attitudes towards their duties could change dramatically if they suspect that they might in due course be deprived of their just desserts.

Criticism

Nobody likes to be told they are wrong. If a business is to function efficiently, however, it is essential that errors are corrected. Aim to ensure that your staff are as self-critical as possible. Encourage them to come to you with suggestions for improving their daily performance. This will relieve you of much of the need to issue reprimands. On those occasions when it is clearly necessary for you to instigate criticism yourself, avoid being too direct in your approach. Try to begin on a positive note by congratulating them on what has been done well. Ensure that you disapprove of actions rather than people. Criticise in private only.

Delegation

The number of occasions on which you are forced to make criticisms will depend to a great extent on the skill you exercise in delegating tasks in the first place. Preferences for performing particular functions should be clearly noted. Important tasks should only be delegated to those whose aptitudes have been tried and tested through involvement with minor activities.

Recruitment

Recruitment is far from being an exact science. A high degree of subjectivity is invariably necessary in judging whether staff are likely to fit in with a particular working atmosphere or perform their duties to required standards. The following guidelines should, however, prove useful to most small businesses.

1. Remember that any attempts to rush your selection procedures are more than likely to backfire. The wrong choice can cost you thousands of pounds in time and money. It will also mean that you have to go through the whole recruitment process again.
2. The trade press can provide a particularly cost-effective medium for recruitment advertising.
3. The more clearly your advertisement defines exactly what you are looking for, the less time you will waste in having to weed out unsuitable applications. Remember that time is money: a few extra pounds spent on obtaining the size of advertisement you require could be repaid many times over.
4. Half an hour should be sufficient time in which to conduct an interview with shortlisted candidates. Ensure, however, that you are free from interruptions. Get your secretary to handle all incoming enquiries.
5. A candidate's application form should provide an adequate basis on which discussions can be conducted.
6. Try to act as naturally as possible. It is important that you get the candidate to relax. It is the human being who you may be working with, not his or her initial airs and graces.
7. Try to ask open-ended questions so that your candidate does as much of the talking as possible. This will enable you to evaluate communication skills as well as give you as broad an insight as possible into personality and past experience.

8. You will probably find that you make a subconscious decision concerning a candidate's suitability during the opening few minutes of an interview. Do not allow this to prevent you from conducting a thorough and unbiased examination.

9. Always take up references to confirm that details of previous employment have been correctly stated. If seeking a personal opinion on a candidate from previous employers remember that they are likely to be more forthcoming when talking in private over the phone than when asked to commit their views in writing.

Reward

People cite a wide number of reasons for doing their chosen job. Status, personal satisfaction derived from the work involved and contact with other people are all commonly quoted. The fact remains, however, that most people go to work because they have to in order to survive financially. The basis on which they are remunerated is thus in most cases by far the single most important factor in determining whether they take up or remain in a position.

The following points should receive due consideration from the smaller business person:

1. More often than not staff and applicants for positions are aware of the terms and conditions common to a particular industry. Quality staff will thus always be difficult to attract and retain if salaries and perks are not broadly in line with those available elsewhere.

2. The basis on which all payments are to be made must be clearly understood by both employer and employee. If members of staff are ever owed money due to them every effort must be made to correct the matter. An explanation as to why the situation was allowed to arise should be provided together with suitable apologies.

3. Some form of profit-sharing can do much to increase loyalty and productivity from staff.

Commission versus salary

The two basic alternatives available for rewarding a sales force are commission and salary. For the smaller business person whose sales force may be limited to a handful of telesales operators, a commission basis can prove particularly suitable. In fact, a great many companies conduct successful telesales operations on a commission-only basis. The following points should be borne in mind when deciding to opt for commission, salary or a combination of both.

Commission

1. Commissions are a variable expense. They do not have to be paid when no business is produced.
2. Commission can provide vital motivation for a sales person to put his or her selling time to the most effective use. This is particularly important in the case of telesales which can often prove highly repetitive and tedious. When commission constitutes much less than a quarter of an overall remuneration package, however, its effect as an incentive tends to be minimal.
3. A sales person working entirely on commission can often be difficult to manage. Because he or she is effectively self-employed instructions can be resented.
4. Firms operating on a commission-only basis often find it difficult to recruit staff, because candidates do not relish the prospect of going without pay when being trained. The situation tends to be less critical in the case of telesales, however, as training can often be conducted in a matter of days or even hours.
5. The prospect of obtaining commission can induce a sales person to oversell, ie try to get orders at virtually any cost. This can have severe repercussions in the long term.
6. Much depends on the skill with which commission levels are set.

Salary

1. A straight salary system is far easier for an employer to administer than a scale of commissions.
2. The expense is fixed, even when no business is forthcoming.
3. The security of a regular income can do much to sustain morale when business temporarily slackens or new territories are being developed.
4. Salaries are difficult to cut and can make sales people hard to get rid of.
5. The prospect of a salary increase is only a very limited incentive for a sales person to maximise productivity.
6. Salary increases can appear unjust.

Points to remember

- Remember that listening is just as important as speaking clearly.
- Try to make people feel important.
- All dealings with staff must be based on total honesty.
- Always criticise in private.
- Encourage staff to be self-critical.
- Never rush selection procedures.
- Try to suppress initial sub-conscious decisions when interviewing.

10
Getting the Best Out of Yourself

Most people find that sitting at a desk is much more comfortable than being out on the road. The practice provides immunity from bad weather, adverse traffic conditions and time spent waiting to see prospective customers who fail to keep their appointments. Considerations of comfort, however, are rarely the primary motivation for wishing to be in the office. Cost-effectiveness is the main benefit. Sales result from contact with decision-makers. If such contact can be made without a personal visit to their premises the number of decision-makers who can be approached in any one working day will be immeasurably greater.

Time

Cost-effectiveness will always depend on the way that time in the office is employed. One of the greatest mistakes that business people make is failing to recognise that time is a commodity. To achieve successful time management it is essential to view time with the same commercial attitude as any other aspect of business. Time is limited, especially for busy entrepreneurs. We only have a fixed amount available every working day, so it is important to come to terms with the fact that every hour and minute at our disposal have their price. Unlike many other commodities, units of time cannot be replaced. Every time a minute is wasted a price has been paid that cannot be refunded.

Nobody in their right mind willingly pours money down the drain. However, many self-employed people think nothing of wasting time. When they do so they are in fact simply wasting money. A sole trader who is paying himself only £200 for a 50-hour week is charging his business £4 an hour for his services. So whenever he fritters away the odd quarter of an hour he has lost his business £1. It would have been better employed backing a horse. At least he would have had a chance of winning.

The factors that contribute to making the most of your time in your working life are many and varied and few of them receive adequate attention. Success in getting the best out of yourself can make as significant a contribution to profitability as success in many of the more obvious challenges involved with running a business. Let us briefly explore some of the major areas that need to be considered.

Planning your time

Many people who are 'frantically busy' accomplish little. This is because they have not learned to make effective use of their time. Putting in long hours is no guarantee that results will be achieved. Careful planning of available time is the key to success.

Always make a point of devoting a few minutes at the end of each working day to planning the next one. Put your plans in writing and stick to them. This will prevent you trying to perform too many different tasks at the same time. Many people waste much of their time trying to determine which of several tasks should have priority. Setting clear objectives can also help your subconscious powers to switch on to the issues at stake.

When you prepare your schedules ensure that you leave ample time for unforeseen developments. Allocate your time on a basis that gives due attention to your most important clients. A well-established maxim in business – the Pareto Principle – states that 80 per cent of your sales come from 20 per cent of your customers. Those 20 per cent of your customers should thus occupy the bulk of your time. Decide which tasks are worthy of your own attention and which need to be delegated.

Don't be afraid to take breaks. If you are working hard they are essential. Frequent brief breaks – a few minutes every hour, for example – will always be more effective than longer ones taken less often. Try to minimise the possibility of distractions. Interruptions can be extremely costly. Not all can be avoided. You can, however, make sure that as many people as possible – especially your personal friends – know those times of day when it is convenient to phone you. There is also much to be said for setting aside a particular slot each day when you can't be disturbed by anyone under any circumstances. Ask your secretary to take your phone calls during this time or, if you have no secretary, leave your answerphone on. Put a notice on your door saying that you can't be disturbed and explaining when you will be available again. Use this quiet period to deal with the most important matters.

The best time to arrange this quiet period is probably first thing in the morning. This is one time when you are least likely to be disturbed. The others are at lunchtime and during the very late afternoon. It is in the morning that we are normally at our most efficient and capable of concentrating on demanding tasks. During the afternoon performance is often less effective. Even this problem can be overcome by making sure that you assign the less taxing routine duties such as letter writing to the afternoon. By doing this you will also ensure that your entire day's post has arrived.

Many business people waste a great deal of time by being disorganised. The filing of correspondence and other information is often very tedious. It is, however, of paramount importance. A few seconds of filing every day could well save hours at a later date trying to locate a vital document. Any piece of information relevant to your business should be readily available. When a phone call from a customer comes out of the blue all relevant details should be within a few seconds' reach.

Being organised involves knowing where things are as opposed to being impeccably tidy. Those with particularly good memories are often capable of high standards of organisation without great tidiness. There is, though, much to be said for keeping your affairs as tidy as possible. By doing so you will at least convey the impression of organisation to visitors and to members of your staff.

Another notable time waster is undue involvement with problems likely to produce little or no business. If you have a client who is constantly seeking advice but never placing any orders, make a point of being less approachable, however much you enjoy talking to him or her. Unfinished tasks can also be a major problem area. Often more time is spent in deciding when to complete them than in the act of completion itself. Always ensure that if a task is not finished it is entered as the first item for attention on the next day's schedule.

Attitude

A positive attitude is probably the most important attribute of any business person. Most successful people talk and act in a positive manner, however worried they may be inwardly. Nothing is more contagious in an office than the expression of negative feeling. When things are going well it is easy enough to think positively. But when times are hard and optimism is all the more essential it is invariably in short supply. Happiness and self-belief cannot be bought and there is no one single recipe guaranteed to produce a desired state of mind. But many of the subjects dealt with below can have a direct influence on the way that we think.

Health

Business people are always thinking of ways of making money but rarely of ways to stay fit and healthy. Health cannot be bought but many inexpensive steps can be taken to improve it. In due course such measures will also have a financial reward.

Keeping physically fit and eating sensibly can have a beneficial effect on the way time is used and customers are handled. Supplies of energy can be increased, physical appearance enhanced and a general feeling of well-being promoted – to an extent that improves even the way a telephone conversation is conducted.

Sleep

An inadequate night's sleep can severely impair the ability to concentrate. In such a situation the only solution is to take short rests, but not so many that you are prevented from getting to sleep once you get home. Otherwise the situation will become a vicious circle.

Psychological factors, such as stress and other day-to-day problems, play a greater part in impairing sleep than physical ones. However, too much coffee before bedtime is also capable of causing the damage. Caffeine can take a long time to pass through the system. If you drink too many cups of coffee during the early part of the day they can keep you awake at night. Too much alcohol can also have an adverse effect on some of the most valuable sleeping patterns.

Eating just before you retire to bed is also likely to prevent sleep. Always allow a gap of a couple of hours between eating your evening meal and bed. Regular exercise contributes to a good general state of health and is also conducive to restful sleep. Fresh air helps as well. Try to make a point of leaving the window open at night.

Weight and appearance

About one-third of our adult population is currently overweight. In most cases there is no excuse. Carrying extra weight can undermine the way that you feel and detract from your performance during face-to-face situations. The importance of appearance in business can never be underestimated, even if you are spending all day at your desk. On those occasions when contact with outside parties is made, first impressions are vital. Being overweight can also greatly increase your chances of contracting some form of heart disease – a major cause of absence from work.

Stress

It has been estimated that stress-related illnesses are responsible for losing industry and commerce in this country some 30 million working days a year. Smaller firms are particularly exposed to the problem as they often lack the in-depth resources to deal with unexpected pressures.

Some degree of pressure is good for you as the response to it prepares the body for action, but if this response goes on for too long health can be seriously damaged. People differ noticeably with regard to what they find stressful but many of the symptoms are easy to recognise. If you find that you are becoming irritable, that you have started to drink more heavily than usual or that you are having particular difficulty in getting to sleep at night, you may well be suffering from some stress-related complaint.

If you can recognise the cause of your stress, solving the problem should be relatively straightforward. If you cannot it might be worth questioning whether or not your time is being organised efficiently or whether you are taking on more work than you can realistically be expected to cope with. Many people adopt short-term solutions to stress that actually merely serve to prolong and aggravate the problem. Excessive smoking, alcohol consumption and eating are all examples of solutions to be avoided. Relaxation is the best remedy.

If you can get your body to relax your mind will relax as well. Swimming and walking are both superb ways of reducing the tension caused by stress. An interesting hobby – even something as straightforward as reading a good book – can be a valuable way of relaxing your mind. A sense of humour can also provide welcome relief.

Relaxation tapes, which involve deep breathing exercises, have now become widely available. These can be listened to in the office. Should you find that stress is a particular problem, however, it may well be worth developing a more sophisticated method for dealing with it.

A technique known as autogenic training has become increasingly popular as a means of reducing stress. Initially it must be taught by a medically qualified person but after eight to ten lessons patients can do it for themselves in their own offices. There is no need for you to leave your desk for the purpose of taking the lessons as they are available outside office hours. The basic idea is that a particular state of mind known as passive concentration can be achieved in which certain phrases are continuously repeated. Once it has been mastered the method can be used to deal with any stressful situation. Details can be obtained from:

The Centre for Autogenic Training
Positive Health Centre
101 Harley Street
London W1
Tel: 071-935 1811

Back pain

About 7 per cent of the adult population suffers from a bad back at any one given time. Contrary to popular belief, all modern research on back pain testifies to the fact that sedentary workers stand a higher chance of incurring disc problems than manual workers. This is because they weaken their spines through sitting for long periods and are thus particularly vulnerable to sudden strain.

The fact that you never leave your desk puts you very much at risk. Back pain doesn't usually happen all at once. It can accumulate gradually and appear after several years. Continuous changes are very much better for the back than constantly sitting in one position. Try to avoid slouching and aim to maintain a good posture with back upright and head and shoulders straight.

Sitting in the traditional way – with the front of your thighs parallel to the floor and at right angles to your stomach increases the pressure on the lower back fivefold compared with lying down. This pressure can be reduced by about a third by placing a wedge-shaped cushion on your chair so that your backside is higher than your knees – the angle between the front of your thighs and your stomach is increased to approximately 115 degrees. If you are writing or reading try to have the surface of the page inclined upwards to prevent excessive bending over the desk.

There is much to be said for spending a little bit extra when buying your office furniture to secure chairs designed to facilitate good posture seating. It is also a good idea to make sure you have a firm mattress on your bed at home. A third of your life is spent in bed, after all!

Smoking

More and more employers are recognising the need to provide a smoke-free environment for the majority of their employees and to help workers who wish to give up the habit. The costs of smoking to industry are much heavier than most people suppose. Cigarettes do more than cause lung cancer. Indeed, it has been estimated that smoking-related illnesses result in the loss of as many as 50 million working days every year. Smoking can have a detrimental effect on a business by reducing productivity through sickness absences, impairing the health of those who attend work and causing duties to be interrupted when people are actually smoking.

Surveys have shown that those who smoke more than 20 cigarettes a day have twice as much time off work because of illness as non-smokers. Many sufferers of smoking-related illnesses experience years of ill-health and subsequent reduction of their productive capacity. If you smoke you run about twice the risk of a heart attack as a non-smoker. The habit is anti-social and can make you less attractive. Lighting up a cigarette can also convey an unsatisfactory impression to visitors. It can suggest lack of self-control and disregard for others.

Those who find the process of giving up smoking a particular problem should seek assistance from:

ASH (Action on Smoking and Health)
5–11 Mortimer Street
London W1N 7RH
Tel: 071-637 9843

Exercise

Exercise is essential if you are to realise your optimum levels of physical and mental well-being. Many companies are implementing fitness programmes at work because they know that exercise will help their staff to feel and look better, raise their general level of performance and confidence, and help to counter stress.

For those who are desk-bound it is especially important that suitable exercise is taken. Even if your resources do not facilitate a formal in-house programme it is essential that you try to take some form of exercise and encourage your staff to do likewise.

There are obviously some activities, such as sit-ups and press-ups, that can be performed in your office. Nevertheless, considerations of personal hygiene dictate that their use is limited. If these exercises are to be done regularly and strenuously to improve your health they will inevitably make you hot and sweaty, so it is recommended that you concentrate on taking your exercise outside office hours when baths and showers are readily available.

Exercise involves any kind of body movement. If performed regularly the effort of moving your muscles rhythmically creates a greater demand for oxygen in the blood and more work for the heart and lungs. This improves the balance of fatty substances in the bloodstream, lowers the resting blood pressure levels and strengthens the heart muscles. The secret is to select an activity that you enjoy. This will greatly increase the chances of it being performed regularly.

To build up stamina you should choose an exercise which gives your body plenty of movement and is just energetic enough to make you fairly breathless but not gasping for breath. Swimming, jogging, rowing and cycling are excellent stamina-building activities. Vigorous forms of exercise should not, however, be attempted until you have reached a good general level of fitness. The fitter you become, the quicker your body will be able to recover from the effort that has been made.

At the least strenuous level, brisk walking is an excellent stamina-building exercise. A brief walk every morning is highly recommended. Make sure that you take it before you eat your breakfast. This will allow your body to become fully involved without having to answer to the demands of your stomach. A brisk half-hour walk two or three mornings a week will prove more beneficial than a game of squash played once a week. Dancing, gardening and interior decorating are other valuable ways to exercise.

Diet

Some people are greedy by nature while others succumb too easily to the temptations of convenience. The type of food that we eat plays a major part in determining our general state of health. It is always wise to examine labels on prepacked food. The ingredients of any item are provided in descending order of weight. Not all foods are as healthy as their manufacturers would like us to believe.

Almost all food provides some form of energy. This is the fuel necessary to power your bodily processes such as heart beat, breathing, growth and repair. If the amount of energy taken in exceeds the amount used the person concerned will put on weight.

The average citizen does not eat nearly enough fibre and consumes far too much fatty food, sugar and salt.

Fat

Eating too much fat tends to make people overweight and increases the risk of heart disease. Women generally need less fat than men and people who do not take much exercise require less than those who do. One-third of the fat eaten by the average Briton comes from dairy products, mostly butter and milk. A quarter is contained in meat-related products, a further quarter in margarines, cooking fats and oils and a sixth in other foods such as crisps, chocolates, biscuits and cakes.

Don't worry about having the odd binge on sweet food to celebrate special occasions. The contribution this will make to your intake of fat will be negligible in comparison with that which results from your regular eating habits. Good ways of cutting down on everyday consumption of fat include using low fat margarine, skimmed milk, low fat yoghurt instead of cream, eating more fish and chicken and grilling food rather than frying it.

Fibre

Research suggests that the average person needs to increase his or her fibre consumption by around 50 per cent. Food such as dairy products, meat and eggs contain no fibre at all. To increase your intake of fibre eat more beans, brown rice, wholemeal pasta, wholemeal bread, bran, fresh fruit and vegetables. Fruit and vegetables can vary a lot in fibre content but will have some and are also essential for vitamins and minerals. Eat more potatoes baked in their skins rather than boiled potatoes or chips.

Sugar and salt

Most people are unaware of the actual amount of sugar they consume. This is because less than half of their intake comes from the bags of sugar they buy. Sugar contains no useful nutrients other than energy and much of the energy we need can be obtained from other sources. Many people also eat far more salt than they need. There is no need to add salt to your meals. On average we consume about 10 grammes but the majority of the population only actually need one. Medical opinion has traditionally advised that in many cases high salt intake can lead to high blood pressure, although recent studies suggest that this link is not entirely straightforward and other factors may well be involved.

Drink

Try to limit your alcohol consumption. Any man who drinks more than 21 units of alcohol a week is greatly increasing his chance of incurring some form of alcohol-related disease. (One unit equals either half a pint of beer, one glass of wine or one standard measure of spirits.) Late arrival at work, headaches, hangovers and lost driving licences are all capable of severely undermining a business's efficiency. Choose low calorie varieties of soft drinks. See if you can do without sugar in your tea and coffee.

Points to remember

- Time is a commodity. Every minute has its price.
- Always plan the next working day in writing.
- Make use of frequent but short breaks.
- Set aside a quiet period each day when you cannot be disturbed.
- A positive attitude can be a business person's main attribute.
- Never underestimate the importance of appearance in business.
- Remember that sedentary workers have a high exposure to back problems.
- Exercise is essential if performance is to be optimised.
- Eat more fibre and less fat, sugar and salt.
- Keep a watchful eye on your alcohol intake.

Appendix

Part B (General Rules) of the British Code of Advertising Practice (8th Edition December 1988)

Reproduced with kind permission of the Committee of Advertising Practice. Readers should consult a complete copy of the Code to follow up the cross references.

The obligations of the advertiser

1.1 Primary responsibility for observance of this Code falls upon the advertiser, and remains with him even when delegated, for practical purposes, to an advertising agency or other intermediary. (This provision in no way affects the responsibility of advertising agencies, which contract as principals, in their relations with publishers.)

Substantiation

1.2 Before offering an advertisement for publication, the advertiser should have in his hands all documentary and other various evidence necessary to demonstrate the advertisement's conformity to the Code. This material, together, as necessary, with a statement outlining its relevance, should be made available without delay if requested by either the Advertising Standards Authority or the Committee of Advertising Practice.

1.3 Whenever conformity with the Code is a matter of judgement rather than evidence, the advertiser should be prepared to explain without delay, when requested to do so, why he believes his advertisement conforms to the Code.

1.4 An advertisement may be found to be in contravention of the Code if the advertiser does not respond, or delays his response, to such requests from the Authority or the Committee.

Confidentiality

1.5 Subject to their overriding duties to the Courts and to officials with statutory powers to compel disclosure, the Authority and the Committee will always respect any request that genuinely private or secret information supplied in support of an advertisement should be treated in confidence.

All advertisements should be legal, decent, honest and truthful.

Legality

2.1 Advertisements should contain nothing which is in breach of the law, nor omit anything which the law requires.

2.2 Advertisements should contain nothing which is likely to bring the law into disrepute.

(As to the treatment of advertisements apparently in conflict with the law, see Introduction, paragraph 16.)

Decency

3.1 No advertisement should contain any matter that is likely to cause grave or widespread offence. Whether offence is likely to be caused and, if so, of what gravity will be assessed in each case in the light of the provisions of A.3.2 above and of the standards of decency and propriety that are generally accepted at present in the United Kingdom.

3.2 Some advertisements, which do not conflict with the preceding sub-paragraph, may none the less be found distasteful because they reflect or give expression to attitudes or opinions about which society is divided. Where this is the case, advertisers should carefully consider the effect that any apparent disregard of the sensitivities involved may have upon their reputation and that of their product, and upon the acceptability, and hence usefulness, of advertising generally.

3.3 The fact that a product may be found offensive by some people is not, in itself, a sufficient basis under the Code for objecting to an advertisement for it. Advertisers are urged, however, to avoid unnecessary offence when they advertise any product which may reasonably be expected to be found objectionable by a significant number of those who are likely to see their advertisement.

Honesty

4.1 No advertiser should seek to take improper advantage of any characteristic or circumstance which may make consumers vulnerable; as, for example, by exploiting their credulity or their lack of experience or knowledge in any manner detrimental to their interests.

4.2 The design and presentation of advertisements should be such as to allow each part of the advertiser's case to be easily grasped and clearly understood.

Truthful presentation: general

5.1 No advertisement, whether by inaccuracy, ambiguity, exaggeration, omission or otherwise, should mislead consumers about any matter likely to influence their attitude to the advertised product.

Matters of fact
5.2

1. Whenever an advertisement is likely to be understood as dealing with matters capable of objective assessment upon a generally agreed basis, it should be backed by substantiation as required by B.1.2 above. The adequacy of such substantiation will be gauged by the extent to which it provides satisfactory evidence that the advertisement is both accurate in its material details and truthful in the general impression it creates.

2. No advertisement should claim that the account it gives of any facts is generally accepted, or universally true, if there exists a significant division of informed opinion as to how either the accuracy or the truthfulness of that account may properly be assessed.

3. When a factual claim in an advertisement is said to be supported by the results of independent research, the advertiser should be able to show that those responsible for the research accept as accurate his account of it.

4. Advertisements which contain material of the kinds described below are not to be regarded, for that reason alone, as in conflict with the Code's rules on truthful presentation:

a) obvious untruths, exaggerations and the like, the evident purpose of which is to attract attention or to cause amusement and which there is no likelihood of consumers misunderstanding;

b) incidental minor inaccuracies, unorthodox spellings and the like which do not affect the accuracy or truthfulness of the advertisement in any material respect;

c) accurate descriptions of the contents of books and other media of communication in circumstances in which some of the matter so described cannot itself be substantiated. (Publications are urged, none the less, to consider carefully the possibility of harm or distress resulting from their acceptance of such advertisements, particularly where these contain material advocating either unproven remedies for disease or disability, or the employment of consumers' resources in risky ventures.)

5. When the consumer's response to an advertisement is likely to be directly affected by the appearance of a person whose real-life experience it describes – as may happen, for example, in connection

with a charitable appeal – a model should not be used to represent that person unless the advertiser makes it quite clear that this has been done.
6. On the truthful presentation of comparisons, see B. 21 to B. 24 below.

Matters of opinion

5.3 The Code's rules on truthful presentation place no constraint upon the free expression of opinion, including subjective assessments of the quality or desirability of products, provided always that

- it is clear what is being expressed is an opinion;
- there is no likelihood of the opinion or the way it is expressed misleading consumers about any matter in respect of which objective assessment, upon a generally accepted basis, is practicable (if there is, the provisions of 5.2 above apply);
- the advertiser is ready to fulfil his obligations under B.1.3 above (substantiation);
- the advertisement is in conformity with B.3 above (decency); and
- so far as commercial advertisers are concerned, the Code's rules on fair competition are observed (see B.21 to B.24 below.)

Truthful presentation: political claims

6.1 To the extent that any advertisement:

- expresses an opinion on a matter which is the subject of controversy; and
- that controversy involves issues within the areas, broadly defined, of public policy or practice,

then neither that opinion, nor any evidence which the advertisement may include in support or explanation of it, is subject to the provisions of this Code on truthful presentation, except as provided in the remainder of this paragraph.

6.2 Assertions of fact and expressions of opinion which are 'political' in the sense of the preceding sub-paragraph will be required to conform to the provisions of B.5 above if they are made in the context of an appeal for funds or are directly linked to the offer of any product in return for payment.

6.3 All advertisements which contain 'political claims' should:

- be readily recognisable as advertisements;
- cause no confusion as to the identity or status of the advertiser; and

– whenever such information is not otherwise readily accessible, state the advertiser's address or telephone number.

Truthful presentation: quotation of prices

(The following paragraph is retained in this edition of the Code in the form in which it appeared in the Seventh Edition. This is done pending the introduction of a new Code on Price Indications [to be made under the Consumer Protection Act 1987] which was close to completion as this edition of BCAP want to press. To the extent that any of the provisions of the forthcoming Code prove to be incompatible with what follows, they will override the corresponding provisions of this paragraph with immediate effect.)

7.1 The provisions of this paragraph apply to advertisements of all kinds. Where appropriate, therefore, 'price' is to be understood as meaning 'charge', 'fee', etc, and references to the sale of goods are to be understood as being applicable also to the provision of services, facilities, etc in return for payment.

7.2 The Code makes no general requirement that the cost to the consumer of an advertised product should be stated in an advertisement (but see C.X. below so far as advertisements addressed to children are concerned).

7.3 When any indication of cost is given in an advertisement, regard should be paid to the provisions of the following four sub-paragraphs.

Clarity

1. If reference is made in an advertisement to more than one product, or more than one version of a single product, it should be clear to which product or version any quoted price relates.
2. If a product is illustrated, and a price quoted in conjunction with the illustrations, advertisers should ensure that what is illustrated can be purchased for the price shown.

Inclusiveness

3. Except when those addressed by an advertiser are likely to be able to recover VAT, prices should normally be quoted inclusive of VAT. When prices are quoted exclusive of VAT, that fact should be stated with no less prominence than the prices themselves. The same principles apply in the case of other taxes and duties.
4. When an advertised product cannot be purchased unless the consumer is willing to make associated purchases from the advertiser (eg where a case has to be purchased with a camera), the price of the advertised product should normally be quoted on a basis which

includes such unavoidable costs. Where it is impracticable to include such costs in the quoted price, because, for example, they are variable while the price of the advertised product is not, the consumer's liability to pay for them should be stated with no less prominence than the price of the advertised product itself.

On price comparisons, see B.21 and especially B.21.3 below.

Truthful presentation: use of 'free'

8.1 When a product is advertised as being 'free', incidental costs which will necessarily be incurred in acquiring it, and which are known to (or can be accurately assessed by) the advertiser, should be clearly indicated; and when such incidental costs exceed those that would typically arise if a comparable product was bought from a comparable source, the product advertised should not be described as free.

8.2 Advertisers should not seek to recover the cost to them of a product which they describe as free

- by imposing additional charges they would not normally make;
- by inflating any incidental expenses they may legitimately recover (eg cost of postage); or
- by altering the composition or quality, or by increasing the price, of any other product which they require to be bought as a precondition of the consumer obtaining the 'free' product.

8.3 Except in the context of a free trial, the word 'free' should not be used if payment for an advertised product is only deferred.

8.4 Any offer which consists in the giving without cost of one product on condition that another is paid for should normally be temporary, otherwise if such a combination offer is continuous, the use of the word 'free' may become misleading.

Truthful presentation: use of 'up to . . . ' and 'from . . . '

9. Expressions such as 'up to x miles per gallon' and 'prices from as low as y' should not be used if, as a result, consumers may be misled about the extent to which the benefits claimed are in practice attainable by them or are available to them.

Truthful presentation: testimonials and other indications of approval

10.1 In this paragraph 'testimonial' embraces any reference made by an advertiser to the favourable opinion of another in circumstances in which the consumer is likely to give added credence to that opinion because of the ostensible independence of the person or institution said to hold it.

10.2 Except when the opinion quoted is available in a published source, in which case a full reference should be made available on request, the advertiser should be able to provide substantiation for a testimonial in the form of a signed and dated statement, containing any words which appear in the advertisement in the form of a direct quotation, and with an address at which the author of the statement may be contacted.

10.3 Testimonials should not be used unless the advertiser has good reason to believe that they represent the genuine and informed opinion of those giving them.

10.4 A testimonial may become misleading if the formulation of the product concerned, or its market environment, changes significantly after the date on which the testimonial was given. As a general rule, therefore, testimonials should relate only to the product as currently offered.

10.5 The fact that a testimonial is given by a person or body independent of the advertiser is not, in itself, sufficient to demonstrate the accuracy or truthfulness of any claim it may contain about a product; and advertisers should be prepared to provide objective substantiation for such claims in the normal way (see B.1 and B.5 above). They should also ensure that, in all other respects, what is quoted by way of testimonial in an advertisement conforms to this Code.

10.6 When fictitious characters in an advertisement express satisfaction with the advertiser's product, care should be taken to avoid consumers confusing them (or their ostensible experiences) with real people or their experiences.

10.7 Advertisers are reminded that testimonials by persons named or depicted in an advertisement may be employed only when the consent of these persons has been obtained in advance (see further B.17 below).

Royal approval

10.8 Attention is drawn to the provisions governing the use of the Royal Arms and Cipher, and references to the Queen's Award to Industry. (Details may be obtained from the offices of the Lord Chamberlain and the Queen's Award to Industry respectively.)

10.9 The Royal Warrant does not imply either personal endorsement or use of the product concerned by HM The Queen (or such other royal person on whose behalf the warrant is issued) and no suggestion that it does should appear in any advertisement.

Truthful presentation: recognisability of advertisements

11. An advertisement should always be so designed and presented that anyone who looks at it can see, without having to study it closely, that it is an advertisement.

Truthful presentation: identity of advertisers

12.1 Except in respect of

– 'political' advertisements (see B.6 above);
– mail order and direct response advertisements (see C.V1 below); and
– the advertisements of itinerant traders (see C.X1.3 below),

the Code makes no requirement that the name or address of an advertiser be given in an advertisement. (As regards advertisements for sales promotions, see British Code of Sales Promotion Practice.)

12.2 When an advertiser is named in an advertisement, the way in which this is done should not be such as to cause confusion about his identity or mislead as to his status or qualifications.

12.3 In some cases there may be a legal requirement that an advertisement names the advertiser. Advertisers are devised to seek professional advice on this point.

Truthful presentation: guarantees

13.1 In this paragraph 'guarantee' includes 'warranty'.

13.2 Advertisers are urged to take legal advice on any reference they wish to make to a guarantee.

13.3

1. Words such as 'guarantee' should not be used in an advertisement if, in consequence, there is any likelihood of consumers mistakenly believing, when such is not the case, that it is the advertiser's intention to confer on them, or procure for them, a legal right to recompense or reimbursement.
2. Where it is intended that such a legal right be created, it should be made clear to the consumer, before he is committed to purchase, whether his right lies against the advertiser or against a third party

(as it may do, for example, where insurance schemes are used to prolong product warranties).
3. Subject to the provisions of the two preceding sub-paragraphs, there is no objection to the use of 'guarantee' in a colloquial sense ('Guaranteed to cheer you up' of a film, for example).

13.4 When an advertisement offers a legally enforceable guarantee as to the quality, life, composition, origin, etc of any product, the full terms of that guarantee should be available for inspection by the consumer before he is committed to purchase, and should be offered for his retention on purchase.

13.5 If the applicability of any guarantee is subject to a substantial limitation (eg one-year; parts only), the nature of that limitation should be given adequate prominence in advertisements referring to the guarantee.

13.6

1. When he uses a phrase such as 'money-back guarantee', the advertiser should be ready to make a full refund of the purchase price to a dissatisfied customer at any point during the expected life of the product, unless a shorter period of time was stated in his advertisement. The payment of such a refund may reasonably be made dependent upon the return of the unsatisfactory product. On mail order advertisements see further C.VI below.
2. Money-back guarantees should not be offered in respect of medicines or by betting tipsters.

Truthful presentation: availability of advertised products
14.1

1. Except in circumstances a) in which the advertisement makes clear that any advertised product is subject to a limitation on availability, or b) in which such a limitation is inherent in the nature of the product (eg theatre tickets), advertisers should be able to show that they have reasonable grounds for supposing that they can supply any demand likely to be created by their advertisement.
2. Products which cannot be supplied should not be advertised as a way of assessing potential demand.
3. Advertisers will be required, in the event of challenge, to demonstrate that they took adequate steps to monitor the adequacy of stocks of all products mentioned in an advertisement between its creation and publication.
4. Advertisers, when advertising on behalf of a number of outlets,

should be able to demonstrate that they have used their best endeavours to ensure that the offers contained in their advertisement have been adequately explained to those outlets and that each has sufficient stock to service them properly.

5. When it becomes clear that an advertised product is not available in sufficient quantity to meet demand, immediate action should be taken by the advertiser to ensure that any further advertisements for the product are properly amended or withdrawn.

Switch selling

14.2 An advertisement may be regarded as misleading if an advertiser's salesmen seriously disparage or belittle the article advertised, recommend the purchase of a more expensive alternative, indicate unreasonable delays in obtaining delivery or otherwise seek to put difficulties in the way of its purchase.

All advertisements should be prepared with a sense of responsibility to the consumer and to society.

Fear and distress

15.1 Without good reason, no advertisement should play on fear or excite distress.

15.2.1. When an appeal to fear is properly made in an advertisement – as, for instance, when it is made with the object of encouraging prudent behaviour – the fear evoked should not be disproportionate to the risk addressed.

15.2.2. An advertisement should excite distress only in circumstances in which the seriousness and importance of the subject matter unarguably warrant such an approach. Distress should never be occasioned merely in pursuit of an attempt to attract attention, or to shock.

Violence and anti-social behaviour

16.1 Advertisements should neither condone nor incite to violence or anti-social behaviour.

16.2 Advertisements for weapons and for items, such as knives, which offer the possibility of violent misuse should avoid anything, in copy or in illustration, that may encourage such misuse.

Protection of privacy and exploitation of the individual

17.1
1. Except in the circumstances noted in paragraphs 17.2 to 17.5 below,

advertisements should not portray or refer to any living persons, in whatever form or by whatever means, unless their express prior permission has been obtained.
2. 'Refer' in the preceding sub-paragraph embraces reference to a person's possessions, house, etc in any manner which unambiguously identifies their owner to prospective readers of the advertisement.

17.2 The circumstances in which a reference or portrayal *may* be acceptable in the absence of prior permission, are the following:

– generally, when the advertisement contains nothing which is inconsistent, or likely to be seen as inconsistent, with the position of the person to whom reference is made, and when it does not abrogate his right to enjoy a reasonable degree of privacy;
– in the special case of advertisements the purpose of which is to promote a product such as a book or film, when the person concerned is the subject of that book, film, etc.

A complaint from a person represented, that an advertisement falling within either of these exclusions is none the less offensive, harmful or humiliating, will be weighed by ASA or CAP when deciding whether the advertisement concerned is within the spirit of the Code.

The applicability of these two exceptions to the general rule is further considered in sub-paragraphs 17.3 to 17.5 below.

17.3 It follows from the above that complaints from those who occupy positions or exercise trades or professions which necessarily entail a high degree of public exposure, such as actors, sportsmen and politicians, can be entertained only

– when it can reasonably be argued that the advertisement concerned suggests some commercial involvement on their part which is of a kind likely to be generally perceived as inconsistent with their status or position; or
– when the effect of the advertisement is to substantially diminish or to abrogate their right to control the circumstances or terms upon which they may exploit their name, likeness or reputation on a commercial basis.

17.4 The use of crowd or background shots, in which individuals or their possessions, houses, etc are recognisable, is not regarded under the Code as inconsistent with the right of such individuals to enjoy a reasonable degree of privacy, provided that there is nothing in the depiction which is defamatory, offensive or humiliating. Advertisers should be ready to withdraw any advertisement in respect of which they receive a reasonable objection on such grounds from a person affected.

17.5 Advertisements in which reference may properly be made to members of the Royal Family include:

- those which incorporate a reference to royal approval which satisfies the provisions of B.10.8 and B.10.9 above;
- those for which express permission has been granted by the Lord Chamberlain's office;
- those for, or depicting, products such as stamps or commemorative items which have received royal approval; and
- advertisements for books, films, articles and the like which deal with a member or members of the Royal Family.

17.6 It is not regarded as contrary to the principle set out in 17.1 above for unsolicited advertising material to be addressed to a consumer personally.

17.7 References to individuals with whom the advertiser is personally acquainted, and which he has no reason to suppose will be resented, are not regarded as infringements of the privacy of such individuals, but should be withdrawn if any reasonable objection is received.

17.8 Advertisers should seek to avoid unnecessary offence to the susceptibilities of those connected in any way with deceased persons depicted or referred to in any advertisements.

Unsolicited home visits

18. When an advertiser intends to call on those who respond to his advertisement, with a view to making a sale, he should either make this clear in the advertisement or should explain his intention in a follow-up letter. In both cases, respondents should be given an adequate opportunity to refuse the salesman's call and the advertiser should help the respondent to communicate his decision by providing either a reply-paid postcard or instructions as to how to make telephone contact. (See also the Financial Services Act 1986 in respect of investment advertising.)

Safety

19.1 As a general rule, advertisements should not show or advocate dangerous behaviour or unsafe practices except in the context of the promotion of safety. Exceptions may be permissible, in circumstances in which emulation is unlikely. Special care should be taken with advertisements directed towards or depicting children or young people (see further CX below).

19.2 There should be no suggestion in any advertisement

– that there is a 'safe' level for the consumption of alcohol; or
– that a product can mask the effects of alcohol in tests on drivers, and
  all advertisements for breath test products should include a prominent
  warning on the dangers of driving after drinking.

19.3 The alcohol content of some 'low alcohol' drinks is none the less
such as to make it unwise to consume them in quantity before driving or
engaging in any other activity for which complete sobriety and
command are needed. Advertisers should take care that such drinks are
not advertised in any way which may lead to such inappropriate
consumption.

(And see, on the advertising of alcoholic drinks in general, Section
CXII below.)

Children

20. Advertisements should contain nothing which is likely to result in
physical, mental, or moral harm to children, or to exploit their credulity,
lack of experience or sense of loyalty (see further CX below).

**All advertisements should conform to the principles of fair
competition generally accepted in business.**

Comparisons

(The following paragraph is retained in this edition of the Code in the
form in which it appeared in the Seventh Edition. This is done pending
the introduction of a new Code on Price Indications (to be made under
the Consumer Protection Act 1987) which was close to completion as
this edition of BCAP went to press. To the extent that any of the
provisions of the forthcoming Code prove to be incompatible with what
follows, and particularly with the requirements of sub-paragraph 21.3,
they will override the provisions of this paragraph with immediate
effect.)

21.1

1. So that vigorous competition may not be hindered and that public
   information may be furthered, comparisons, whether between
   products themselves or between the prices of products, are regarded
   as in conformity with this Code provided that such comparisons do
   not conflict with the requirements of this paragraph and of the
   following three paragraphs (B.22 to B.24). This is so even in
   circumstances in which the comparison identifies a competitor of the
   advertiser or that competitor's product.

2. The requirements of this paragraph and of paragraphs B.22 to B.24 apply also, where relevant, to comparisons made by an advertiser between two or more of his own products, or between the price at which one of his products is sold, and the price at which it was sold, or is to be sold.

21.2 Advertisements containing comparisons should deal fairly with any competitors involved and should be so designed that there is no likelihood of a consumer being misled. In particular:

- it should be clear with what the advertised product is being compared, and upon what basis;
- the subject matter of the comparison and the terms in which it is expressed should not be such as to confer any artificial advantage upon one product as against another (this is of especial importance in comparisons between branded and unbranded products and between natural products and substitutes for them);
- claims to objectively superior or superlative status should be expressed in terms which accurately reflect the extent and the nature of the evidence available to substantiate them; and
- no claim that a competitive product is generally unsatisfactory should be based on the highlighting of selected advantages only of the advertised product.

21.3

1. When a price for a product is quoted in a way which may suggest that the product concerned is a bargain, and particularly when one price is compared directly with another, there should be no exaggeration of the extent to which a purchaser may benefit by buying at that price.
2. Specifically, comparisons may be regarded as unfair when one (or both) of the elements in the comparison have been artificially selected or manipulated so as to maximise any apparent saving.
   On the quotation of prices generally, see B.7 above.

Denigration

22.1 Advertisers should not seek to discredit the products of their competitors by any unfair means.

22.2 In particular, no advertisement should contain inaccurate or irrelevant comments on the person, character or actions of a competitor.

22.3 Nor should an advertisement describe or show the products of a competitor as broken or defaced, inoperative or ineffective. The only exception to this rule is where the description or depiction is based upon the outcome of fair comparative tests to which the advertiser's product also has been subjected and the results of such tests are stated.

Exploitation of goodwill

23. Avertisements should not exploit the goodwill attached to the trade name or mark of another, or his advertising campaign, in any fashion which may unfairly prejudice his interests.

Imitation

24. No advertisement should so closely resemble another advertisement as to be likely to mislead or confuse.

Further Reading from Kogan Page

A complete list of Kogan Page titles for the smaller business is available on request from the address on page 4. Three general books likely to be of interest are:

Getting Sales
Marketing Without a Marketing Budget
Successful Marketing for the Small Business

Chapter 3. Using the Post

How to Market Books, Alison Baverstock 1990
Running Your Own Mail Order Business, Malcolm Breckman, 1987

Chapter 4. Using the Telephone

Telemarketing: Strategies for Implementation and Management,
    Michael Stevens, 1990
Telemarketing Basics, Julie Freestone and Janet Brusse, 1990
Selling by Telephone: Tested Techniques to Make Every Call Count,
    Len Rogers, 1986

Chapter 5. Advertising

Effective Advertising, H C Carter, 1985
A Handbook of Advertising Techniques, 2nd edition, Tony Harrison,
    1989
How to Advertise, Kenneth Roman and Jane Maas, 1983
Running a Successful Advertising Campaign, Iain Maitland, 1989

Chapter 6. Getting Free Publicity

Decent Exposure, Vincent Yearley, 1991
Be Your Own PR Man, 2nd edition, Michael Bland, 1987
How to Promote Your Own Business: A Guide to Low Budget Publicity,
    James W Dudley, 1987
How to Write Articles for Profit and PR, Mel Lewis, 1989

Promoting Yourself on TV and Radio, M Bland and S Mondesir, 1987
Principles of Public Relations, Harold Oxley, 1989

Chapter 7. Obtaining Publicity Through Intermediaries
The subject is touched on in some titles listed under Chapter 6.

Chapter 8. Equipping the Office
How to Run an Office, Jennifer Rowley, 1991

Chapter 9. Getting the Best Out of Other People
Effective Employee Participation, Lynn Tylczak, 1990
Getting the Best Out of People, David Robinson, 1988
How to Motivate People, Twyla Dell, 1989

Chapter 10. Getting the Best Out of Yourself
Fit for Work: A Practical Guide to Good Health for People Who Sit on the Job, Scott Donkin, 1990. This book is also applicable to Chapter 8.
How to Get More Done, John and Fiona Humphrey, 1990
Make Every Minute Count, Marion E Haynes, 1988

Index